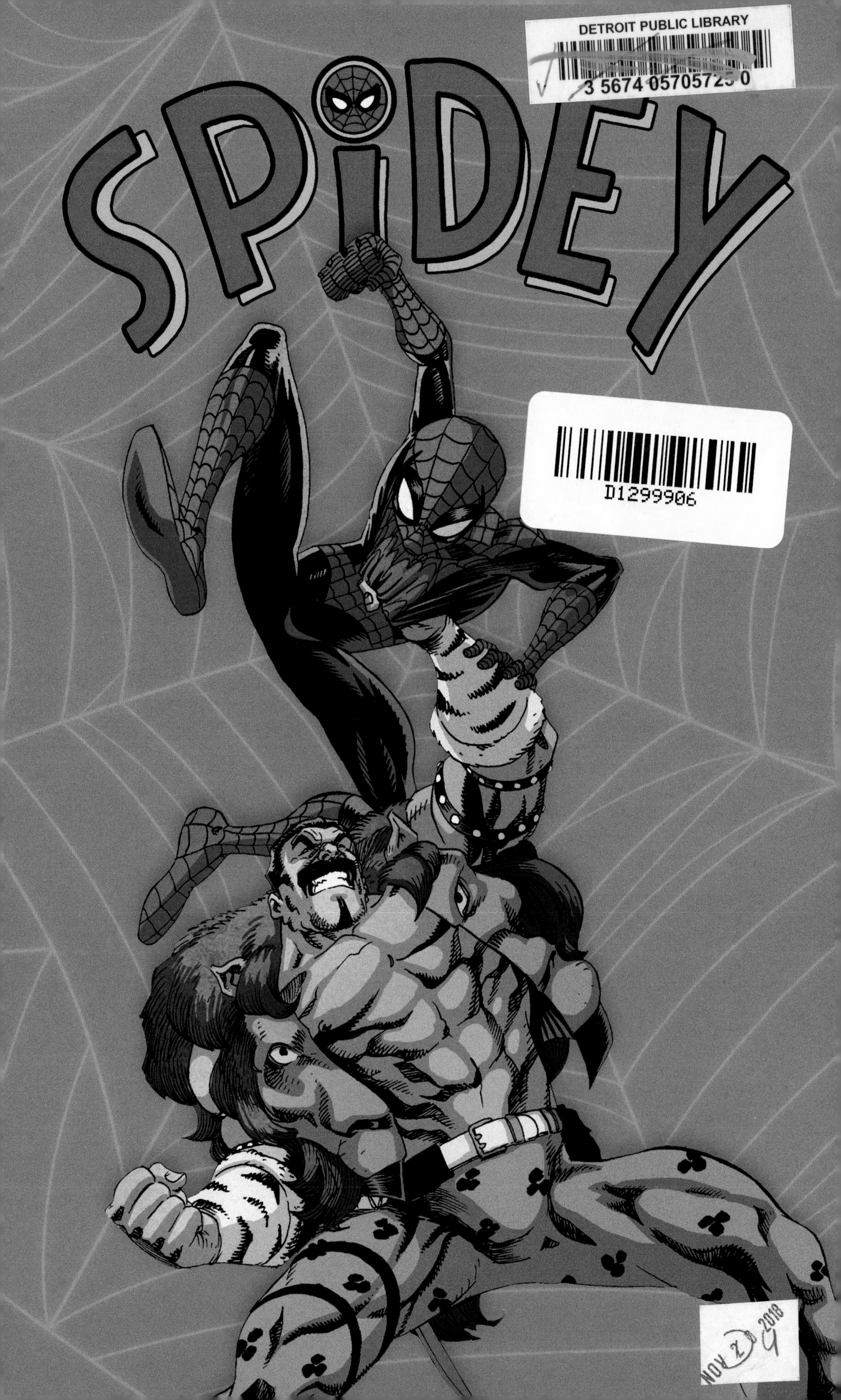
SPIDEY

AFTER-SCHOOL SPECIAL

ROBBIE THOMPSON
WRITER

ANDRÉ LIMA ARAÚJO (#7) &
NATHAN STOCKMAN (#8-12)
ARTISTS

JIM CAMPBELL
COLOR ARTIST

VC's TRAVIS LANHAM
COLOR ARTIST

KHARY RANDOLPH & EMILIO LOPEZ
COVER ART

DARREN SHAN
EDITOR

NICK LOWE
EXECUTIVE EDITOR

———————— SPIDER-MAN CREATED BY **STAN LEE** & **STEVE DITKO** ————————

COLLECTION EDITOR: **JENNIFER GRÜNWALD**
ASSOCIATE MANAGING EDITOR: **KATERI WOODY**
ASSOCIATE EDITOR: **SARAH BRUNSTAD**
EDITOR, SPECIAL PROJECTS: **MARK D. BEAZLEY**
VP PRODUCTION & SPECIAL PROJECTS: **JEFF YOUNGQUIST**
SVP PRINT, SALES & MARKETING: **DAVID GABRIEL**
BOOK DESIGNER: **ADAM DEL RE**

EDITOR IN CHIEF: **AXEL ALONSO**
CHIEF CREATIVE OFFICER: **JOE QUESADA**
PUBLISHER: **DAN BUCKLEY**
EXECUTIVE PRODUCER: **ALAN FINE**

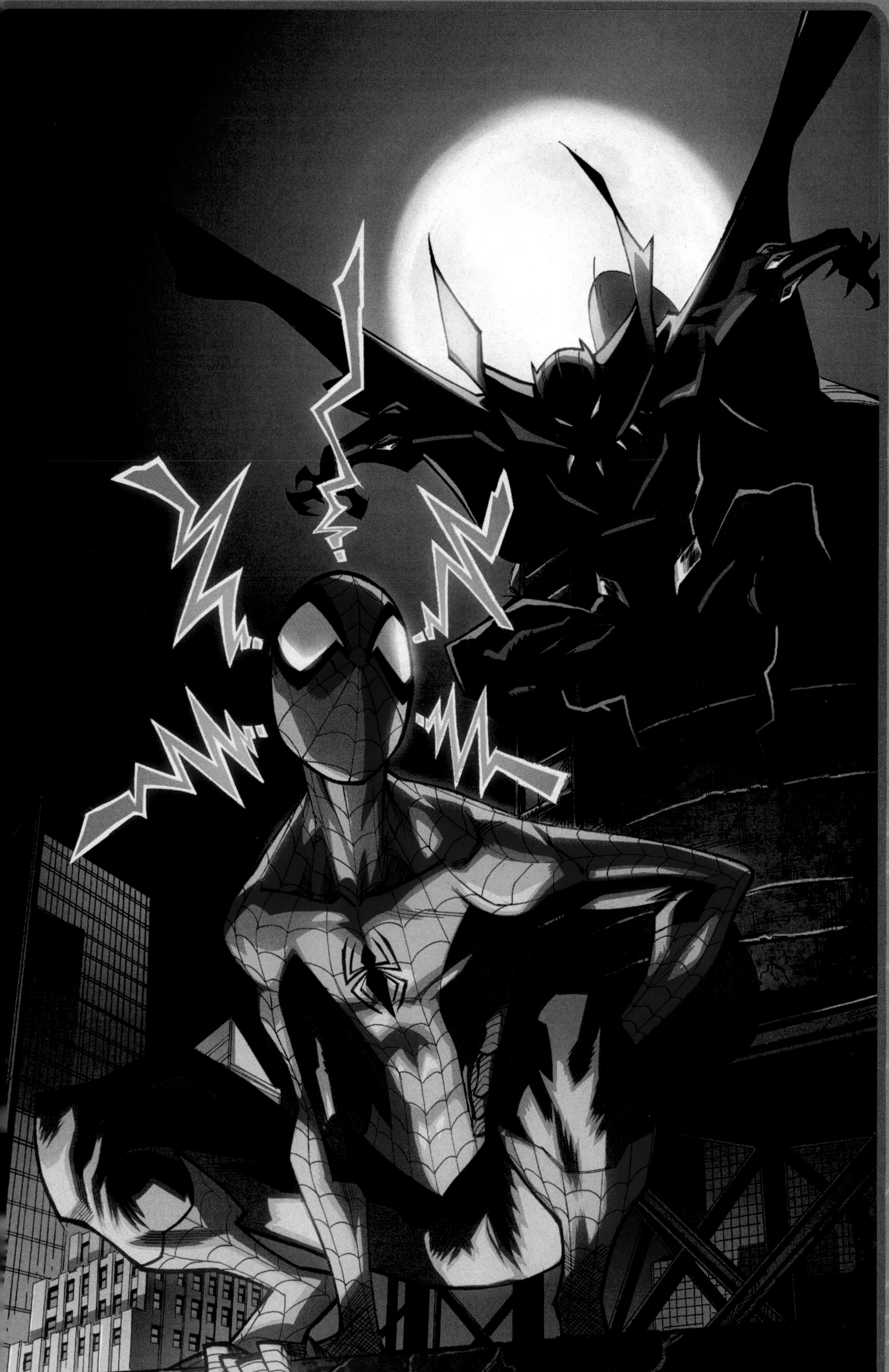

7

MY NAME IS PETER PARKER.

A WHILE BACK, I GOT BIT BY A *RADIOACTIVE* SPIDER.

THE BITE GAVE ME INCREDIBLE POWERS.

WHICH I TOTALLY MISUSED.

HELP! STOP THAT GUY!

GOOD LUCK WITH ALL THAT.

AND WHILE I WAS BUSY BEING FOOLISH...

...I LOST MY UNCLE BEN.

HE ALWAYS TOLD ME THAT WITH GREAT POWER, THERE MUST ALSO COME GREAT *RESPONSIBILITY.*

SO, I PUT MY COSPLAY SKILLS TO GOOD USE, BUILT SOME WEB-SHOOTERS.

AND BECAME...

SPIDER

ORIGIN ART BY *NICK BRADSHAW* & *JIM CAMPBELL*

ARE YOU LISTENING? IS THIS THING ON?

HI.

HOW ARE YOU? I HOPE YOU'RE DOING BETTER THAN ME.

'CAUSE I'VE HAD A WEIRD WEEK.

HOW WEIRD, YOU ASK?

C'MON, *ONE* OF YOU ASKED.

WELL, IT WAS SO WEIRD THAT...

...THESE GUYS?

WEREN'T THE WEIRDEST PART OF SAID WEEK.

OKAY, *HE* WAS KINDA WEIRD.

Monday.

I'D LIKE TO SAY SCHOOL WAS WEIRD.

NICE SHIRT, PARKER.

OH, OOF, THANKS, FLASH!

KICK ME!

Tuesday.

BUT THIS?

NICE BOOKS, PARKER.

Wednesday.

NICE HAIR, PARKER.

SADLY NORMAL.

Thursday.

FORTUNATELY, MY "BEST PAL" FLASH THOMPSON WAS OUT SICK ON THURSDAY.

BEST DAY OF THE WEEK!

NOW, I KNOW, I KNOW. I'M *SPIDEY*. MY WEEK *COULD* HAVE BEEN LIKE THIS...

Dream Monday.

NICE SHIRT-- WHOA!

BUT THIS...

Dream Tuesday.

NICE BOOKS-- WHOA!

...IS NOT MY LIFE.

Dream Wednesday.

UH, HEY, PETER, HOW'S IT GOING...?

NOT EVEN A LITTLE.

Dream Thursday.

I HAVE TO KEEP MY POWERS SECRET. ALONG WITH MY TRUE IDENTITY.

SO, THIS IS ALL PART OF MY NORMAL ROUTINE. FRIDAY IS WHEN THINGS GOT WEIRD...

Actual Friday.

YOU WANT ME TO DO *WHAT?*

I WANT YOU TO TUTOR FLASH.

FLASH *THOMPSON.* THE GUY WHO HATES MY GUTS. THE GUY WHO HATES *EVERYONE'S* GUTS-- EXCEPT YOURS, OF COURSE.

I KNOW HE CAN BE A JERK SOMETIMES.

SOMETIMES?

I THINK YOU TWO COULD ACTUALLY GET ALONG. ESPECIALLY IF YOU HELP HIM KEEP HIS GRADES UP SO HE CAN STAY ON THE FOOTBALL TEAM. WHAT DO YOU THINK?

POSSIBLE ANSWERS:

A. NO THANK YOU.

B. ARE YOU TRYING TO PLAY PEACEMAKER OR TRYING TO GET ME KILLED AND ARE YOU AND FLASH LIKE A THING OR JUST FRIENDS OH MAN SOMEONE STOP ME PLEASE--

C. I'D RATHER CHEW OFF MY OWN HAND.

D. *ARE YOU CRAZY?!?!*

CAN I THINK ABOUT IT?

YOU'RE THE *BEST.*

I'M THE *WORST.*

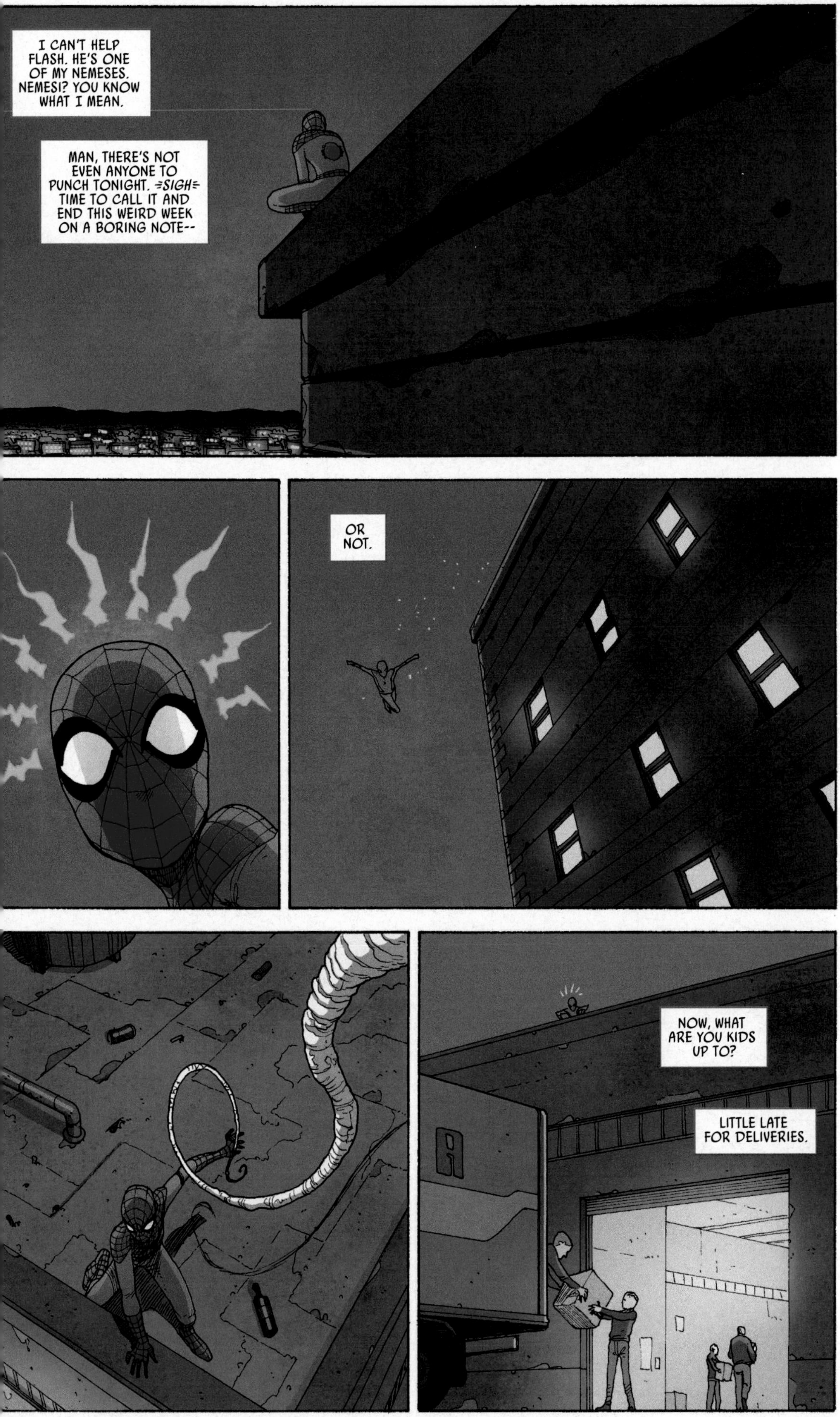

I CAN'T HELP FLASH. HE'S ONE OF MY NEMESES. NEMESI? YOU KNOW WHAT I MEAN.
MAN, THERE'S NOT EVEN ANYONE TO PUNCH TONIGHT. =SIGH= TIME TO CALL IT AND END THIS WEIRD WEEK ON A BORING NOTE--
OR NOT.
NOW, WHAT ARE YOU KIDS UP TO?
LITTLE LATE FOR DELIVERIES.

OKAY, LET'S TAKE A PEEK AND SEE--

UM, IS IT JUST ME...

...OR DID EVERYONE DISAPPEAR?!

TRAP DOOR...? AWESOME.

I MEAN, IT'S PROBABLY A HORRIBLE NIGHTMARE DOWN THERE, BUT STILL. TRAP DOOR!

WORK WITH ME, PEOPLE.

THIS IS ONE OF THE MANY TIMES IN MY SHORT, PERHAPS ABOUT-TO-END, CAREER THAT I WISH I COULD CALL FOR BACKUP.

'CAUSE DOWN THERE...

...ARE A LOT OF FACES TO PUNCH.

BETTER GET CRACKING. IT'S NOT LIKE THEY'RE GOING TO PUNCH THEMSELVES.

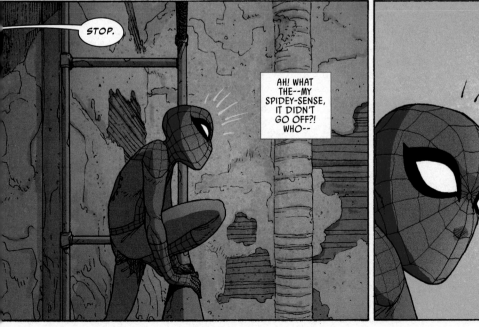

STOP.

AH! WHAT THE--MY SPIDEY-SENSE, IT DIDN'T GO OFF?! WHO--

OH. THAT EXPLAINS IT.

BLACK PANTHER

A.K.A. T'CHALLA, KING AND PROTECTOR OF WAKANDA.

I HAD HEARD WHISPERS OF A SPIDER-THEMED HERO PATROLLING THE CITY OF NEW YORK.

WAIT, *HE'S* HEARD OF *ME?!*

BUT I WOULD ADVISE YOU TO CEASE YOUR CURRENT COURSE OF ACTION, YOUNG MAN.

THOSE MEN DOWN THERE MUST ANSWER TO *ME*.

THEY'RE FRIENDS OF YOURS?

THEY ARE THIEVES. THEY HAVE STOLEN SOME OF WAKANDA'S PRIZED COMMODITY--

VIBRANIUM?! *WOW.* THE RARE WAKANDAN METAL WITH ALL KINDS OF CRAZY PROPERTIES--IT CAN ABSORB SOUND, AND--WAIT, *WHAT?* I'M TALKING TOO MUCH, AREN'T I? I TALK TOO MUCH WHEN I'M--

... YOUR REPUTATION WAS THAT OF *INEXPERIENCE.* BUT... YOU'VE CLEARLY DONE YOUR HOMEWORK.

UM... THANKS? WAIT, WHO SAID I WAS INEXPERIENCED--

MY SPIES HAVE BEEN TRACKING THIS STOLEN VIBRANIUM ALL OVER THE WORLD.

NOW, HEED MY WORDS, YOUNG MAN, AND GO HOME TO YOUR--

WHAT? OHHHHH... YOU WERE STILL TALKING. MY B.

KEEP GOING. I'M SURE I'LL BE ABLE TO HEAR YOU OVER THE PUNCHING AND SCREAMING.

AMERICANS.

ALL RIGHT, LET'S SHOW THIS GUY HOW THINGS GET DONE AROUND--

WHOA!

YOU'RE DEAD, SPIDE-- GAH!

PANTHER IS *FAST!* FASTER THAN ME.

IT'S LIKE HE KNOWS WHERE THEY'RE GOING BEFORE THEY DO.

THAT'S BECAUSE I CAN SENSE WHERE MY OPPONENTS ARE ABOUT TO STRIKE *BEFORE* THEY DO.

OH, MAN. I SAID THAT LAST ONE OUT LOUD, DIDN'T I? BEAT DOWN.

OR WAIT: CAN YOU READ MINDS, TOO?

YOU OUTER-MONOLOGUED. OCCUPATIONAL HAZARD.

IT'S LIKE MY SPIDEY-SENSE, BUT WAY FASTER. AND MORE INTUITIVE.

ANY CHANCE YOU WERE BITTEN BY A RADIOACTIVE PANTHER?

DON'T BE ABSURD.

RIGHT. POWERS FROM A RADIOACTIVE BITE. TOTALLY ABSURD.

WHAT I DO, YOUNG SPIDER, IS LISTEN.

I LISTEN TO MY SURROUNDINGS, AND THEN--

WHAZZ

BOOOOM

WHAM

PUNCH

KRAK

WHOA. THAT WAS AWESOME. DID YOU SEE THAT?

OF COURSE HE SAW THAT--

DUDE, INNER MONOLOGUE.

CURIOUS. A PORTION OF WHAT WAS STOLEN IS MISSING.

WELL, I'M HAPPY TO HELP--

GAHH, WHAT THE--!

BLACK PANTHER. YOU ARE TENACIOUS...

...BUT YOU ARE NO MATCH FOR THE HAND OF **THE KLAW!**

THE *HAND* OF THE KLAW? RESPECTFULLY, ISN'T THAT A LITTLE REDUNDANT?

I SHOULD HAVE KNOWN YOU WERE BEHIND SUCH A SHAMEFUL ACT.

YOU WOULD BE WISE TO REMEMBER OUR *LAST* ENCOUNTER. YOUR SIMPLE SOUND DEVICE IS NO MATCH FOR THE BLACK PANTHER.

STAND DOWN, KLAW, OR PREPARE TO BE BEATEN AGAIN!

OH, I *PREPARED* ALL RIGHT...

WOOOOOM

...PREPARED TO *DESTROY* YOU.

THE MISSING VIBRANIUM FROM THIS BATCH? I USED IT TO FASHION MY *NEW* KLAW.

HOW DOES IT *SOUND*, PANTHER?

ARE YOU *LISTENING?* CAN YOU HEAR EVERYTHING PERFECTLY NOW?

GRRAAAHH!

WITH THE REST OF THIS VIBRANIUM I'LL FASHION *DOZENS* OF KLAWS. AND SOON WAKANDA WILL ANSWER TO ME-- NOT SOME PATHETIC KING!

WOOooooooOOOOOOOOOOM

WOW, THAT REALLY HURT.

EARS ARE RINGING.

EVERYTHING IS RINGING.

AM I TALKING TO MYSELF TOO LOUD?!

AT LEAST I'M INNER-MONOLOGUING AGAIN.

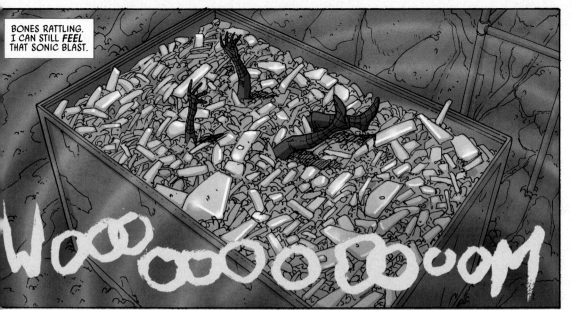

BONES RATTLING. I CAN STILL *FEEL* THAT SONIC BLAST.

WOOOOOOOOOOOOM

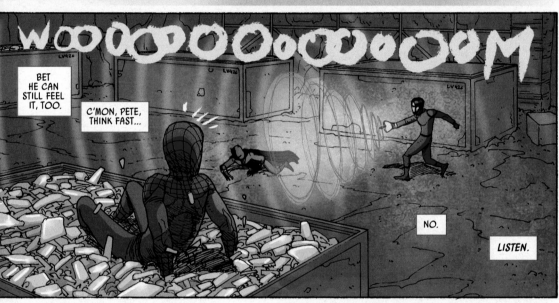

WOOOOOOOOOOOOOM

BET HE CAN STILL FEEL IT, TOO.

C'MON, PETE, THINK FAST...

NO.

LISTEN.

WOOOOOOOO)OOO

THESE ARE VIBRATING AT A SUB-ATOMIC LEVEL. HENCE THE NAME. YOU CAN FEEL IT. *HEAR* IT.

VIBRANIUM CAN *ABSORB* SOUND. WHICH MEANS...

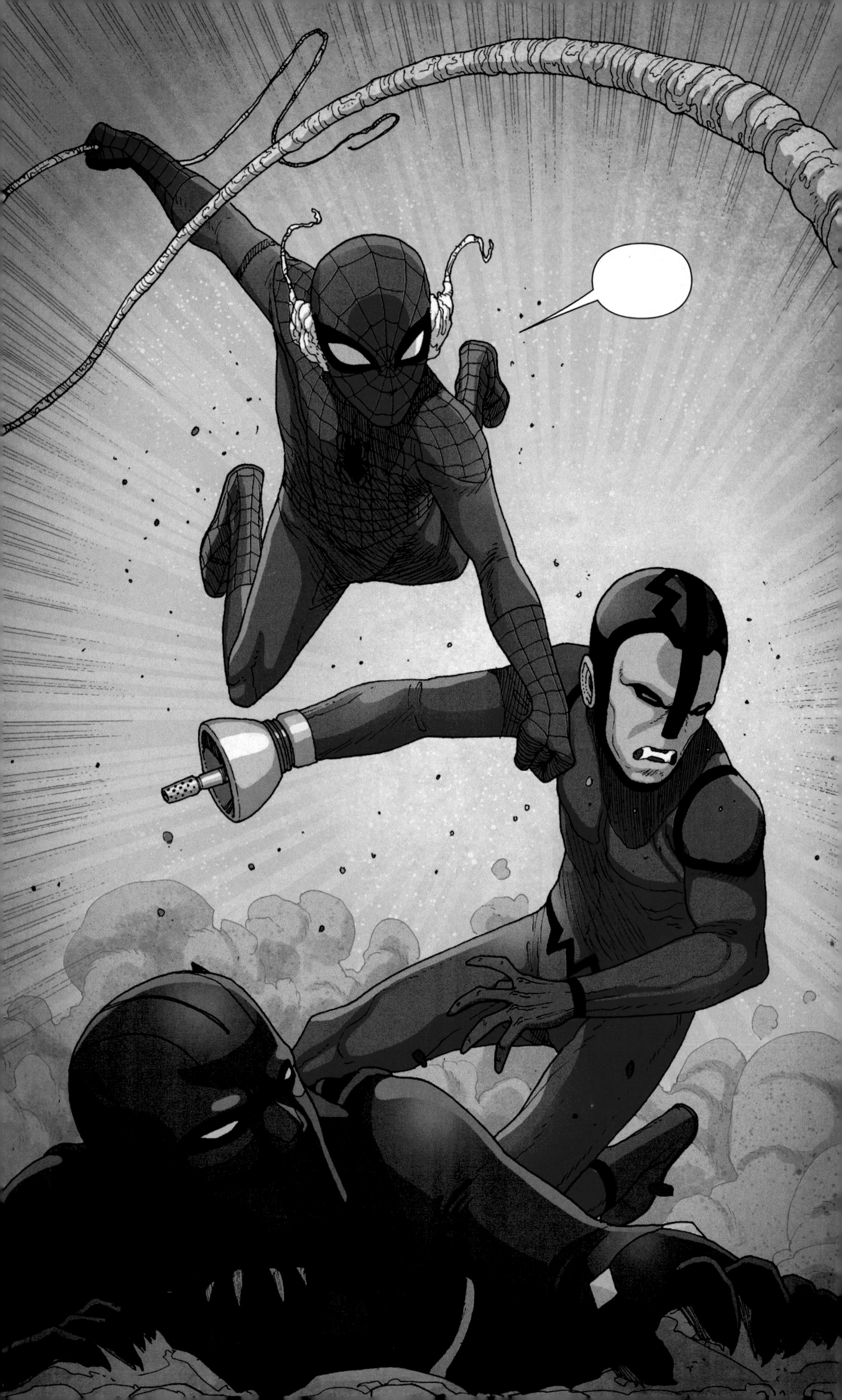

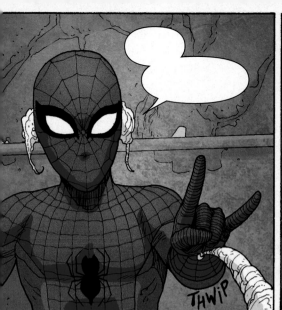

THWIP

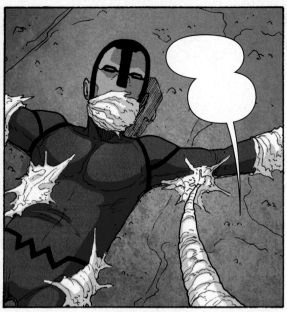

...RIGHT... SORRY, MY BAD.

WAS I YELLING? I WAS YELLING WASN'T I?

SCREAMING, ACTUALLY. YOU SHOULDN'T CURSE SO MUCH, YOUNG MAN.

I WON'T TELL IF YOU WON'T TELL, DEAL?

SO, WHAT HAPPENS TO THEM?

I TURN THEM OVER TO S.H.I.E.L.D. AND RETURN THE VIBRANIUM TO WHERE IT BELONGS: WAKANDA.

YOU ARE WELCOME TO VISIT MY GREAT NATION ANY TIME.

SERIOUSLY? *THANKS.* AND, *UH,* THANKS FOR THE FIGHTING ADVICE. YOU SURE YOU WEREN'T BITTEN BY A RADIOACTIVE PANTHER?

I AM QUITE SURE.

NOW, YOU SEE, *LISTENING* IS ALWAYS THE ANSWER, YOUNG SPIDER. IN COMBAT, AND IN ALL ASPECTS OF LIFE.

WHEN YOU LISTEN, YOU OPEN YOUR MIND TO A WORLD OF POSSIBILITY. A WORLD WHERE THE MUNDANE BECOMES--

LISTENING. GOT IT.

SEE YOU IN THE NEXT TEAM-UP!

AMERICANS.

Monday.

BLACK PANTHER'S RIGHT, OF COURSE. I GUESS THERE'S A REASON HE'S KING AND ALL.

AND SO...I BRACE MYSELF FOR ANOTHER WEIRD WEEK. BUT THIS TIME...I LISTEN.

Tuesday.

...AND LISTEN.

...I RESPECT NOT FIGHTING BACK. I DO.

NON-VIOLENT PROTEST, I GET.

BUT THERE'S NO REASON FOR YOU AND FLASH TO HATE ONE ANOTHER.

Wednesday.

AND THERE'S NO REASON FOR HIM TO FAIL, LIKE, ALL OF HIS CLASSES.

I CAN HELP IN HISTORY, YOU CAN HELP IN MATH...MAYBE HE SQUEAKS BY IN THE REST.

SO... WHAT DO YOU SAY?

Thursday.

BEHAVE!

Friday.

HIM? SERIOUSLY?

HIM. SERIOUSLY.

IT'S A PACKAGE DEAL, FLASH. WE BOTH HELP YOU, OR NEITHER OF US HELP YOU. TAKE IT OR LEAVE IT.

I DON'T KNOW WHY SHE'S FRIENDS WITH YOU, PARKER.

FRIENDS WITH *ME?!* WHY IS SHE FRIENDS WITH YOU, YOU PIG-HEADED--

NO. LISTEN.

WHAT DO YOU HEAR? I HEAR THE SOUND OF SOMEONE *NOT* BEATING ME UP.

YEAH, I WONDER ABOUT THAT, TOO.

PEACE AT LAST. WELL, FOR THE TIME WE STUDY TOGETHER AT LEAST.

LATER TODAY FLASH WILL GIVE ME A WEDGIE. BUT I NOTICE THAT HE PULLS HIS WEDGIE *JUST* A BIT. THANKS, FLASH. AND THANKS, GWEN.

AND HEY, THANK YOU: FOR LISTENING.

SEE YOU ALL SOON. ♥ ANDRÉ LIMA ARAÚJO.

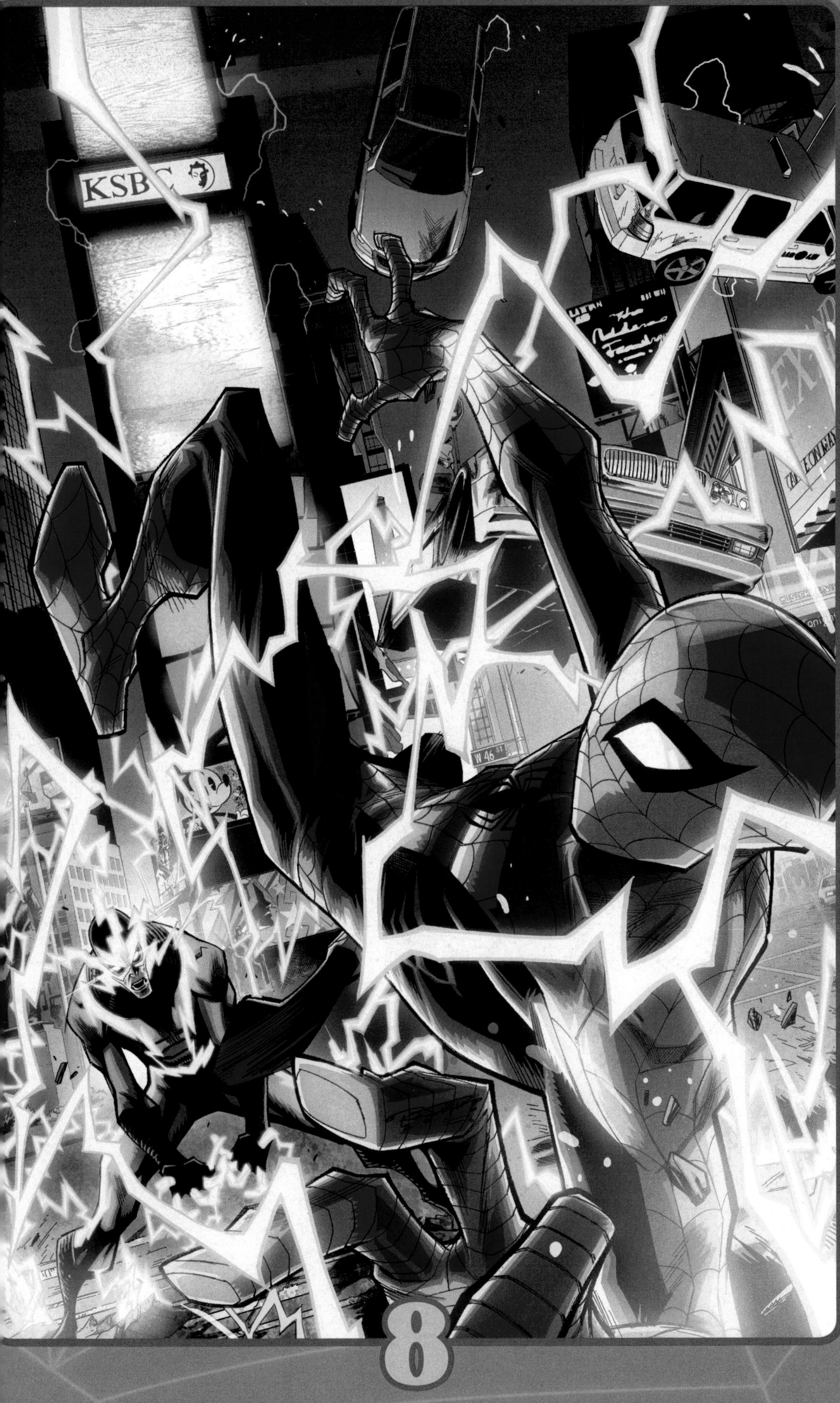
KSBC
W 46 ST

8

I KNOW WHAT YOU'RE THINKING.

BUT THIS *ISN'T* A DATE.

MOJO MOVIES

CLASSICS MONTH

RAIDERS OF THE LOST ARK

RAIDERS OF THE LOST ARK

DIT.CO.

ONLY REASON A GEEK LIKE ME EVEN *KNOWS* GWEN STACY IS BECAUSE WE TUTOR EACH OTHER FOR SCHOOL.

I WISH THEY'D MAKE ONE OF THESE MOVIES SET IN NEW YORK. THERE'S SO MANY ARCHAEOLOGICAL ADVENTURES TO BE HAD RIGHT *HERE!*

I MEAN, WE'RE STANDING ON TOP OF MILES AND MILES OF TUNNELS--WHO KNOWS WHAT'S DOWN THERE! DINOSAURS? BURIED TREASURE? ALIENS?

THAT RIGHT THERE IS WHY YOU'RE AN AWESOME HISTORY TUTOR.

YEAH, WELL, IT TAKES TWO TO TANGO.

THIS *ISN'T* A DATE.

RIGHT?

THIS MAY, OR MAY NOT, BE MY SEVENTH TIME SEEING THIS MOVIE.

HAH--ME, TOO!

SAW IT *TWICE* WITH FLASH.

=*SIGH*= FLASH THOMPSON. HER POTENTIAL BOYFRIEND.

DEFINITELY NOT A DATE.

HOW *ARE* THINGS GOING WITH FLASH?

FINE.

WE'RE JUST FRIENDS.

WAIT, WHAT--

KZZT

UM, IS IT ME, OR DID THE LIGHTS JUST GO OUT...?

I'M SURE EVERYTHING'S FINE--

--AH!

YOU KNOW WHAT? I'LL JUST GO CHECK.

BACK IN TWO SHAKES...

OKAY, THIS IS A PROBLEM.

BUT, IF I MAY ASK: HOW *BIG* A PROBLEM?

'CAUSE I MAY, OR MAY NOT, BE ON A DATE.

I JUST *HAD* TO ASK...

BLACKOUT!

COULD JUST BE A POWER OUTAGE.

THAT'S A THING THAT HAPPENS.

BUT THAT WOULDN'T SET OFF MY SPIDEY SENSE...

C'MON, FOCUS, PETER...

AH, THERE YOU ARE. TOUGH TO FIND A SPIDER...

...IN ALL THIS DARKNESS.

ELECTRO.

I REALLY SHOULD HAVE PUT THAT TOGETHER SOONER.

HEY, SPARKLES. LONG TIME.

YOU REALLY WANT TO TANGLE AGAIN?

"IT USUALLY DOESN'T END WELL FOR YOU...

"...PLUS, SINCE WE LAST WENT AT IT?

"I'VE MADE A FEW ADJUSTMENTS.

...BAD FOR YOU.

BRAVO, SPIDER.

BUT AS YOU'RE ABOUT TO SEE...

"WHICH IS GOOD FOR ME..."

...I'VE MADE SOME ADJUSTMENTS AS WELL!

GHHAHHHH!

...THAT JOLT...

...WENT THROUGH THE *GROUNDING* IN MY WEBBING... *AND MY SUIT*...

TONIGHT WILL BE OUR *LAST* ENCOUNTER, SPIDER. TONIGHT THE WORLD SEES YOU FOR WHAT YOU REALLY ARE: *NOTHING.*

...CAN'T FEEL MY...

WHAM

...ANYTHING...

I'VE TAKEN ALL THE ELECTRICITY IN MANHATTAN, SPIDER.

KABOOM

SAVED IT ALL UP *JUST* FOR YOU.

TONIGHT, YOU *DIE!*

DAILY BUGLE NEW YORK'S FINEST DAILY PAPER

KRAK

IS THIS BECAUSE I KEEP STOPPING YOU FROM BEING A CROOK?

'CAUSE A SIMPLE THANK-YOU CARD WOULD SUFFICE.

OH, NO-- THAT SIGN!

PETER...? PETER...?!

BOOM

OH, NO!

DAILY BUGLE

NEW YORK'S FINEST DAILY PAPER

AH!

YOU OKAY?

I WAS UNTIL YOU TACKLED ME.

YOU'RE WELCOME...?

DON'T WORRY, I GET THAT ALL THE TIME.

RAIDERS OF THE LOST ARK

WHOA. HEY.

HEY. NICE TO SEE YOU AGAIN.

YOU REMEMBER ME?

WHO COULD FORGET YOU?

LISTEN, I APPRECIATE THE HELP, BUT THERE'S A HOMICIDAL-SLASH-ELECTRICAL MANIAC ON THE LOOSE, SO--

BUT I CAN'T FIND MY FRIEND, PETER.

"FRIEND", HUH?

DEFINITELY. NOT. A. DATE.

DON'T WORRY--YOUR FRIEND, IS UH, ACTUALLY HELPING THE POLICE GET PEOPLE INSIDE.

WHAT, WHERE...?

HE'S, UH...RIGHT THERE.

YOU CAN'T SEE 'CAUSE IT'S TOO DARK BUT HE'S THE REAL MVP OKAY GREAT SEEING YOU AGAIN GOTTA GO!

PETER'S AN AWESOME GUY, BY THE WAY. FIRM HANDSHAKE. GREAT HAIR.

OKAY, BYE AGAIN!

YOU DONE PLAYIN' HERO, CHUMP?

C'MON, SPARKLES. LET'S NOT DO THIS.

WHATEVER IT IS THAT WE'RE DOING.

IT'S CALLED BEATING YOU DOWN, GENIUS.

OKAY, GOTTA GET THIS DUMMY AWAY FROM ACTUAL HUMANS.

IF ONLY WE WEREN'T FIGHTING IN THE MOST POPULATED CITY IN THE WORLD...

GAH!

OOOF!

...MUST BE SOME KINDA BLACKOUT...

...GUESS I'M WALKING...

...GONNA BE LATE FOR THE SHOW...

DOES EVERYONE ELSE SEE STARS RIGHT NOW, OR IS IT JUST ME?

IT'S JUST ME.

WAITASEC.

SUBWAY

I KNOW A PLACE WHERE THERE'S NOBODY.

GWEN, YOU'RE A GENIUS.

SORRY, FOLKS, COMING THROUGH!

AIEEE!

WHAA--!

PLEASE DON'T LET THERE BE A LIGHT AT THE END OF THIS TUNNEL...

YOU THINK YOU CAN HIDE FROM ME?!

HIDE FROM YOU? DON'T BE SILLY.

I'M GONNA NEED YOUR LIGHT.

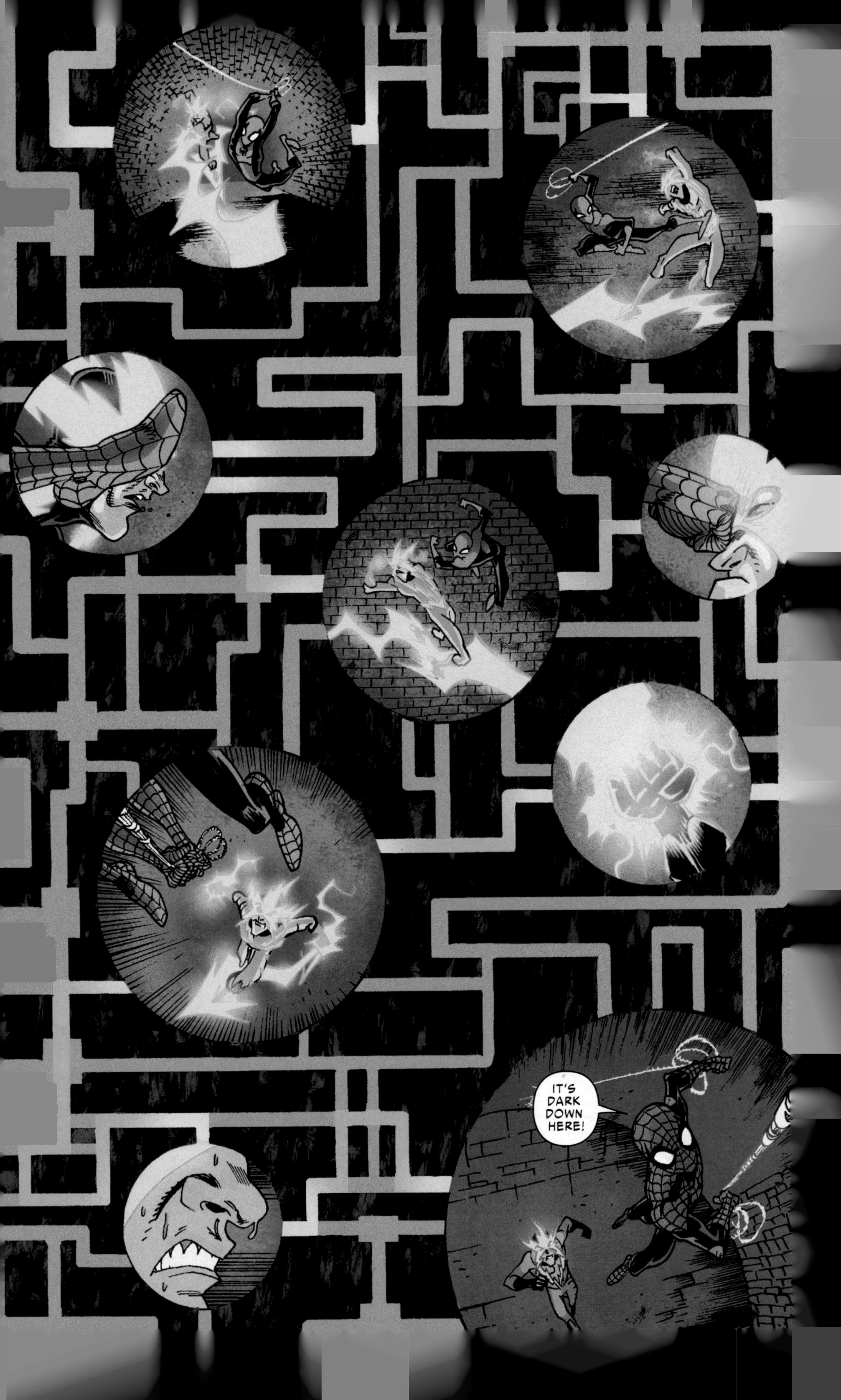
IT'S DARK DOWN HERE!

DON'T SAY IT.

DEAD END, SPIDER.

DUDE.

YOU'RE TRAPPED.

YOU'RE RIGHT.

BUT SO ARE YOU.

BZZZT

TOOK ALL YOUR JUICE JUST TO FOLLOW ME DOWN HERE...

...DOWN HERE, WHERE THERE'S NO PEOPLE...AND MORE IMPORTANTLY...

...NO ELECTRICITY.

WHICH MEANS...

DON'T SAY IT.

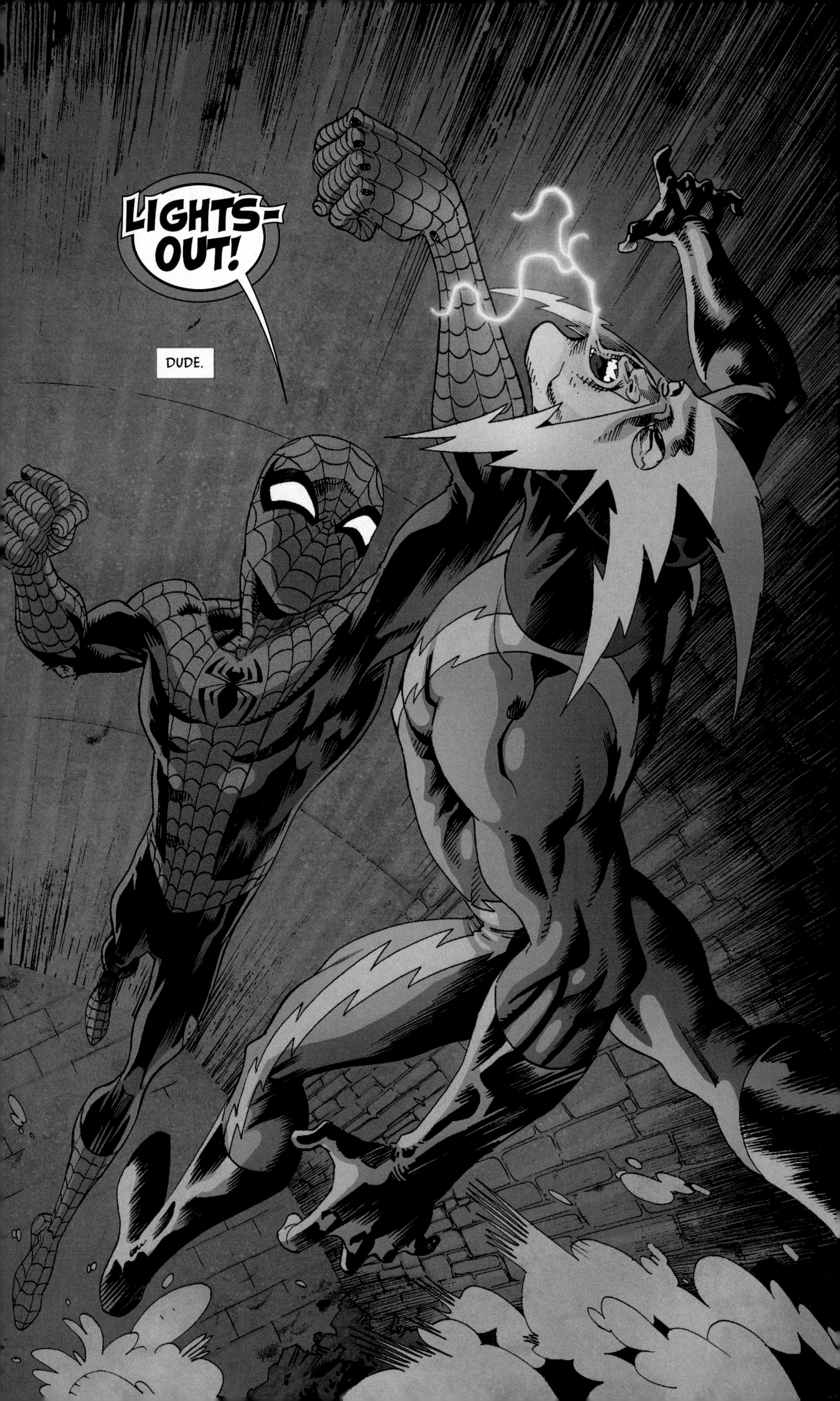
LIGHTS-OUT!
DUDE.

SEE YA AROUND, SPARKLES.

YOU'LL PAY FOR THIS!

HE *SHOULD* PAY FOR THIS--*THE BUGLE* IS RIGHT: YOU'RE A MENACE!

UM...YOU'RE WELCOME...?

SIGH.

ALL RIGHT. BACK TO MY "NOT DATE."

IF I CAN FIND GWEN AT ALL.

PETER, THERE YOU ARE!

YOU OKAY?

YEAH, YOU?

YEAH! I MET SPIDER-MAN!

ME TOO. GREAT GUY. FIRM HANDSHAKE. HE SAID YOU WERE HELPING PEOPLE.

JUST DOING MY PART.

WELL, WHAT YOU DID WAS PRETTY COOL. UM, WHAT YOU DID THAT I DIDN'T SEE AT ALL--

Y'KNOW, WHAT? I DON'T THINK THE POWER'S COMING BACK ON FOR A WHILE AND IT'S GETTING PRETTY LATE.

RAIN CHECK ON THE MOVIE?

SURE.

IT'S A DATE.

PRETTY SURE THEY'RE NOT GONNA LET YOU WEAR THAT GETUP IN JAIL, PAL.

HEY, WHAT THE HECK IS--

BOOOM

WHAT THE...

YOU?!

NOW WHY WOULD YOU HELP ME?

I HAVE A PLAN TO DESTROY SPIDER-MAN, AND I NEED YOUR HELP, ELECTRO.

WHAT KIND OF PLAN?

WELL, TO BE FRANK, IT'S RATHER...

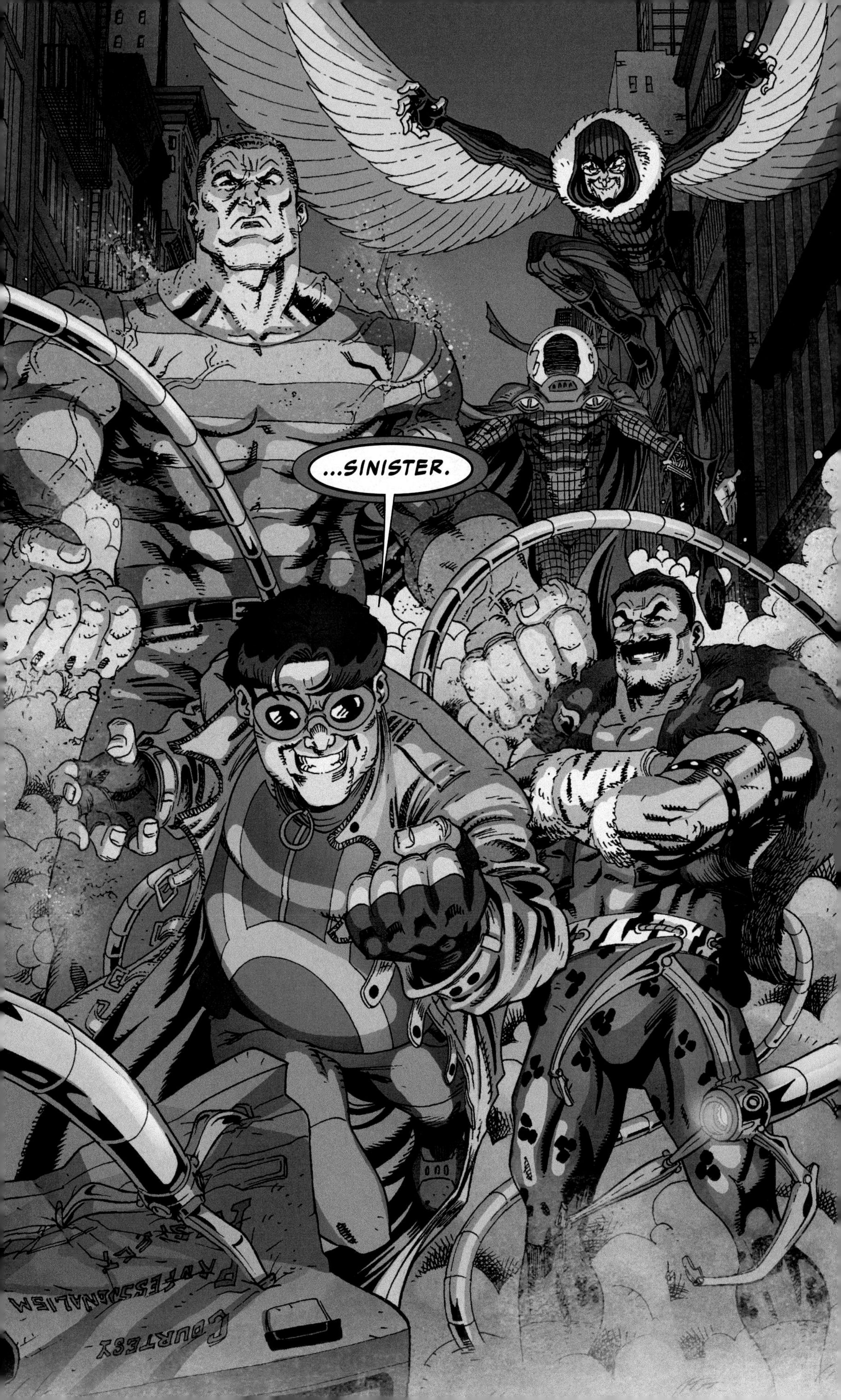
...SINISTER.

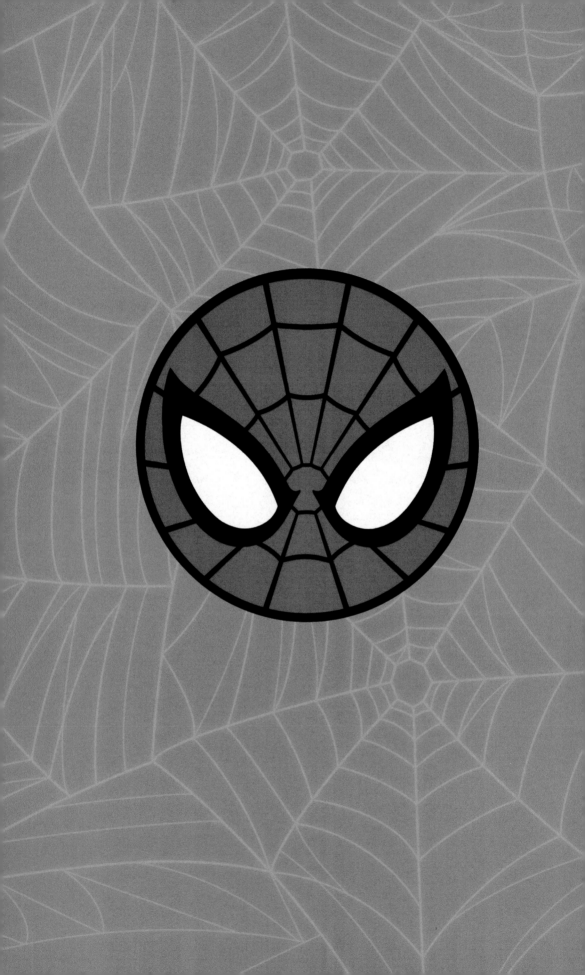

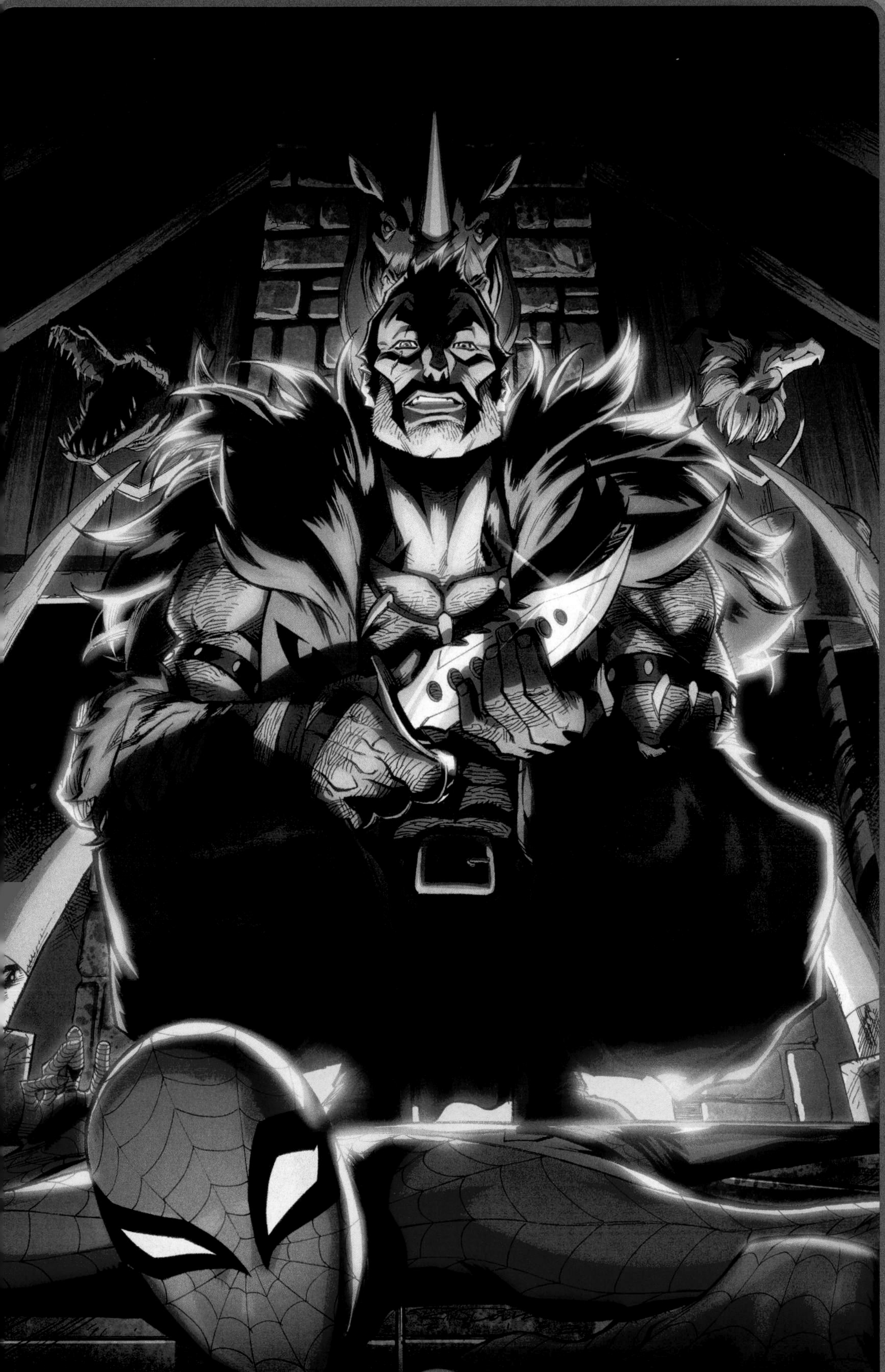

9

TO CATCH A SPIDER!

MY JOB IS AWESOME.

THE ONLY PROBLEM?

IT DOESN'T PAY VERY WELL.

AND BY VERY WELL, I MEAN... AT ALL.

SO, I FREELANCE HERE AT THE *DAILY BUGLE*. SELL PICS OF SPIDEY.

DAILY BUGLE

SPIDEY/GOBLIN PARTNERS?

DAILY BUGLE

THE PROBLEM WITH THE *BUGLE*?

THEY PAY VERY LITTLE.

AND BY THEY, I MEAN... *J. JONAH JAMESON.*

YOU WANT A *RAISE?!* SO DO I!

ONLY REASON I'D BRING YOU ON FULL TIME IS SO I COULD *FIRE* YOU!

J. JONAH JAMESON
EDITOR IN CHIEF

NOW GET OUT OF MY OFFICE AND DON'T COME BACK UNTIL YOU HAVE MORE PICTURES OF THAT *CRIMINAL*, SPIDER-MAN!!

THEY ALSO GIVE ME NO CREDIT. FOR THE PICTURES, OR STOPPING THE GOBLIN.

GOOD TIMES.

AT LEAST THEY HAVE...

...NAH JAMESON
...DITOR IN CHIEF

...AN *ACTUAL* FILM LAB.

NICE TO SEE PEOPLE STILL SHOOTING FILM.

IT'S WHAT MY UNCLE TAUGHT ME ON, RAPHAEL. SO IT'S WHAT I PREFER.

GOOD MAN.

THE BEST. THIS IS HIS CAMERA, ACTUALLY.

MIGHT BE A FEW OTHER SHOTS WORTH A LOOK ON THESE--

HUH. THAT'S FUNNY. NOT SURE WHERE *THIS* OLD ROLL CAME FROM.

LET ME SEE... THIS COMPANY'S BEEN OUT OF BUSINESS FOR YEARS. DO YOU KNOW WHEN YOU SHOT THIS?

NO CLUE.

I'LL PRINT IT FOR YOU ALONG WITH THESE, PARKER. IF JONAH WANTS TO BUY ANYTHING, I'LL GIVE YOU A SHOUT.

FINGERS CROSSED HE BUYS EVERY SINGLE PRINT. IT'S AUNT MAY'S *BIRTHDAY* SOON AND SO FAR ALL I'VE GOT IS A POCKET FULL OF LINT.

CREEEK

IS THAT YOU WITH MY COFFEE, BRANT? I ASKED FOR IT TWO WHOLE MINUTES--

THIS PHOTO...

...WHO TOOK IT?

DAILY BUGLE

SPIDEY/GOBLIN PARTNERS?

WHO ARE YOU SUPPOSED TO BE? PETER PARKER'S AGENT?

TELL YOUR CLIENT HE'S AN IDIOT!

AND THEN REMIND HIM THE BUGLE DOESN'T CREDIT PHOTOGRAPHERS. EVER!

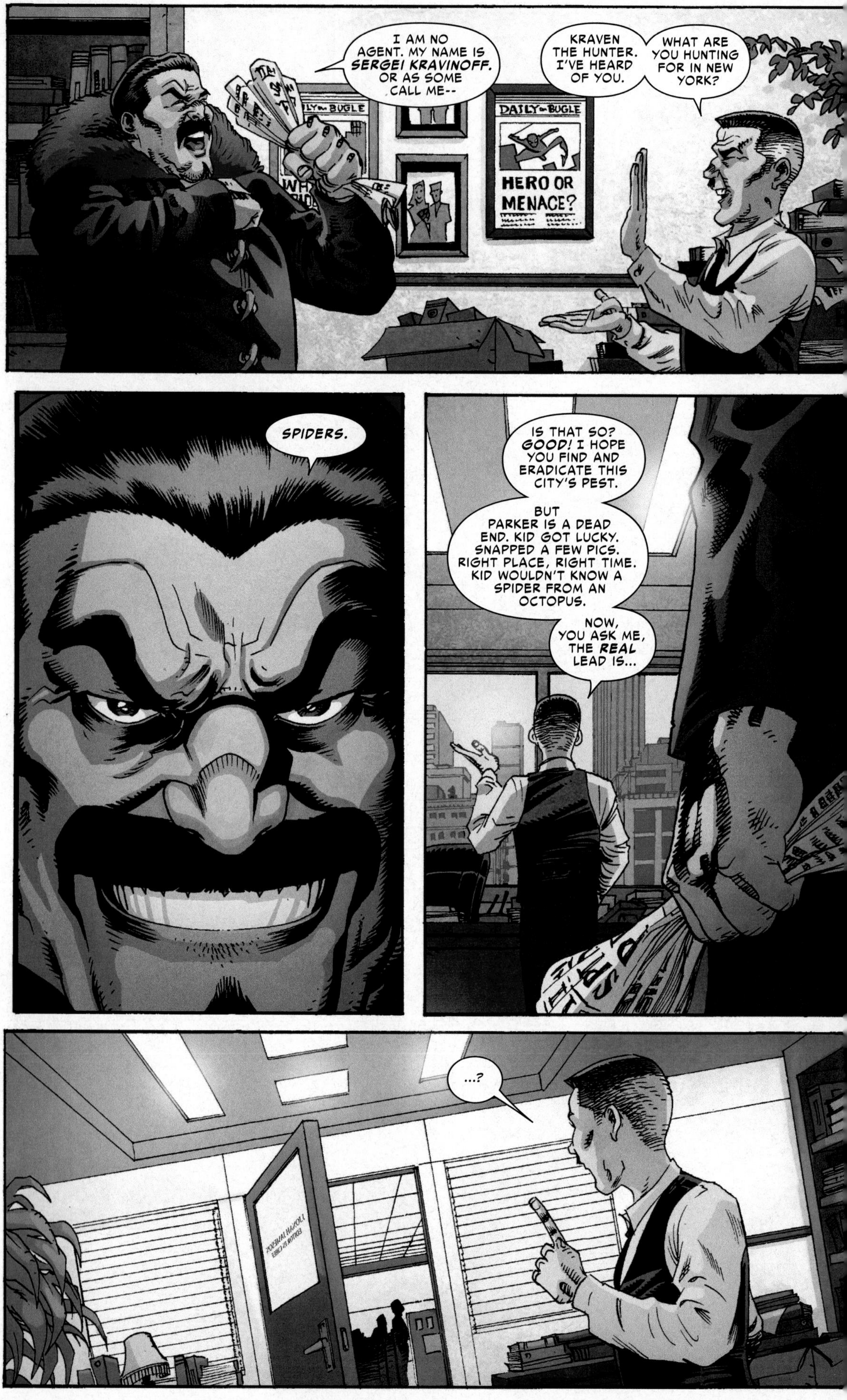
I AM NO AGENT. MY NAME IS SERGEI KRAVINOFF. OR AS SOME CALL ME--
DAILY BUGLE
DAILY BUGLE
HERO OR MENACE?
KRAVEN THE HUNTER. I'VE HEARD OF YOU.
WHAT ARE YOU HUNTING FOR IN NEW YORK?
SPIDERS.
IS THAT SO? GOOD! I HOPE YOU FIND AND ERADICATE THIS CITY'S PEST.
BUT PARKER IS A DEAD END. KID GOT LUCKY. SNAPPED A FEW PICS. RIGHT PLACE, RIGHT TIME. KID WOULDN'T KNOW A SPIDER FROM AN OCTOPUS.
NOW, YOU ASK ME, THE REAL LEAD IS...
...?

AUNT MAY DESERVES *EVERYTHING*...

...WHICH IS TOUGH TO BUY WHEN YOU HAVE *NOTHING*.

$100

$80

MAYBE I CAN TAKE OUT A LOAN. CAN TEENAGERS TAKE OUT--

--AAAAH! *SPIDEY-SENSE.*

PRETTY SURE I'M BEING FOLLOWED.

ONE WAY TO FIND OUT...

THAT'S KRAVEN THE HUNTER!

WE'VE TANGLED BEFORE. IS HE FOLLOWING ME...OR SPIDEY?

REALLY HOPING IT'S NOT ME. PETER-ME. NOT SPIDEY-ME.

Y'KNOW WHAT? LET'S JUST SEE WHAT FURRY'S GOT TO SAY FOR HIMSELF.

KRAV-O, BUDDY, YOU HIDE OUT IN THIS ALLEY, TOO?

KRAVEN THE HUNTER DOES NOT HIDE, SPIDER-MAN!

RIGHT. KRAVEN THE HUNTER HUNTS. ARE YOU HUNTING LITTLE OLD ME? 'CAUSE WE ALL KNOW HOW WELL THAT WENT FOR YOU LAST TIME.

TIMES CHANGE.

OUCH! IS IT JUST ME, OR HAS HE GOTTEN FASTER?

I CAUGHT THE SCENT OF YOUR PHOTOGRAPHER. PETER PARKER.

A FRIEND OF YOURS, OR PERHAPS--

PUNY PARKER? PLEASE.

THAT GUY NEVER GETS MY GOOD SIDE.

PLUS HE MAKES ALL THAT MONEY OFF THOSE PHOTOS, AND NEVER SHARES WITH THE CLASS.

PETER PARKER IS THE WORST.

OKAY, DON'T OVER-SELL IT, PARKER.

HE LED ME TO YOU. SO...

...I AM IN HIS DEBT.

AAAGH!

YUP. HE IS *DEFINITELY* FASTER.

HIS ENHANCED HUNTER-NESS... IT'S LIKE MY SPIDEY-SENSE. WE'RE EACH JUST A STEP AHEAD OF THE OTHER--

--OR, AT LEAST, WE *WERE.*

YOU HAVE HAD AN EXCELLENT RUN, SPIDER-MAN.

I'M NOT REALLY A RUNNER, I'M MORE OF A-- OOOF!

BUT NOW YOUR RUN COMES TO AN *END.*

SERIOUSLY, NOT A RUNNER. NOT EVEN A JOGGER-- GAAHH!

THE ANIMALS YOU KILL, DO YOU EAT THEM, OR DO YOU JUST HAVE THEM STUFFED AND MOUNTED?

I PUT THEM IN MY COLLECTION, OF COURSE.

FINALLY WE HAVE SOMETHING IN COMMON: I HAVE A STUFFED ANIMAL COLLECTION, TOO.

HE'S PULLING HIS PUNCHES.

...I AM IN HIS DEBT.

AAAGH!

YUP. HE IS DEFINITELY FASTER.

HIS ENHANCED HUNTER-NESS... IT'S LIKE MY SPIDEY-SENSE. WE'RE EACH JUST A STEP AHEAD OF THE OTHER--

--OR, AT LEAST, WE WERE.

YOU HAVE HAD AN EXCELLENT RUN, SPIDER-MAN.

I'M NOT REALLY A RUNNER, I'M MORE OF A-- OOOF!

BUT NOW YOUR RUN COMES TO AN END.

SERIOUSLY, NOT A RUNNER. NOT EVEN A JOGGER-- GAAHH!

THE ANIMALS YOU KILL, DO YOU EAT THEM, OR DO YOU JUST HAVE THEM STUFFED AND MOUNTED?

I PUT THEM IN MY COLLECTION, OF COURSE.

FINALLY WE HAVE SOMETHING IN COMMON: I HAVE A STUFFED ANIMAL COLLECTION, TOO.

HE'S PULLING HIS PUNCHES.

PLAYING WITH HIS FUTURE STUFFED ANIMAL.

SOME OF THESE TACTICS ARE NEW.

SOME OF THEM ARE ACTUALLY QUITE SHOCKING.

SORRY NOT SORRY.

GAH-- DUDE. I *JUST* FINISHED KNITTING THIS COSTUME.

IS HE HUNTING?

OR EXPERIMENTING?

IT'S TOO BAD YOUR FRIEND PARKER ISN'T HERE. I'VE LOST HIS SCENT.

OKAY, HE DIDN'T PULL EITHER OF THOSE PUNCHES. OUCH.

I WOULD LOVE HIM TO CAPTURE THE MOMENT OF YOUR DEMISE.

WELL, NICE TO KNOW MY SUIT'S IDENTITY-PROTECTION THERMALS ARE WORKING.

THAT'LL BE A NICE FEATURE FOR WHOEVER PEELS THIS SUIT OFF MY DEAD BODY.

HE OR SHE WILL PROBABLY LIKE THIS FEATURE, TOO.

WHAT...?!

OH COME ON, KRAV-O...

CLK

...YOU LOVE THE SPOTLIGHT!

NOW, I HATE TO BREAK IT TO YOU, BUT, WHILE I'M FLATTERED, I CAN'T BE A PART OF YOUR STUFFED ANIMAL COLLECTION.

PLEASE SEND MY REGRETS TO MR. PICKLES AND BOO-BEAR.

THWIP

THWIP

THAT WAS TOO EASY.

THAT WAS SO EASY.

I'M NOT THAT GOOD.

I GUESS I'M JUST THAT GOOD.

MAYBE I'M JUST LUCKY...

WHAT DO YOU THINK, KRAV-O?

YEAH, I AGREE.

I GOT LUCKY.

"GARBAGE..."

...GARBAGE. MORE GARBAGE.

WHERE'S THE KRAVEN FIGHT?

SIR?

SOME KIDS POSTED BLURRY PHOTOS ON THE INTERNETS. WHERE ARE THE PHOTOS FROM *THAT*, PARKER? KRAVEN TRIED TO RID THIS CITY OF THAT MENACE AND YOU MISSED IT?!

KRAVEN THOUGHT PETER BAILED...SO NO PHOTOS THIS TIME. NO PHOTOS, NO MONEY. NO MONEY, NO GIFT FOR AUNT MAY. AND ONCE AGAIN...

GUESS I BLEW IT, SIR.

GO CHECK IN WITH RAPHAEL, SEE IF HE FOUND ANYTHING ELSE ON YOUR FILM!

I'M NOT PAYING FOR ANY OF THIS GARBAGE!

J. JONAH JAMESON
EDITOR IN CHIEF

SORRY, PETER.

IT'S OKAY. I WAS GRASPING AT STRAWS.

I DID PROCESS THAT OLD ROLL OF FILM, THOUGH.

THANKS, RAPHAEL. I OWE YOU ONE.

NOTHING FOR THE PAPER, BUT MAYBE FOR A SCRAPBOOK?

OH WOW, THESE ARE FROM A FEW YEARS AGO. BACK WHEN...

YOU OKAY?

YEAH, RAPHAEL. JUST REALIZED THERE ARE SOME GIFTS YOU CAN'T PUT A PRICE ON...

I DO NOT LIKE LOSING.

SOMETIMES YOU HAVE TO LOSE IN ORDER TO *WIN.*

I TRIED ALL OF YOU AND YOUR FRIENDS' LITTLE TRICKS.

NONE OF THEM WORKED.

IT'S LIKE I TOLD YOU...

...NOTHING KILLS BETTER THAN A PAIR OF *HANDS.*

WELL...

...I'M IN LUCK THEN, AREN'T I?

BASED ON THESE READINGS... THE SPIDER IS STRONGER AND FASTER THAN I BELIEVED.

I'LL KEEP *EXPERIMENTING.* AND WHEN THE TIME IS RIGHT...

...YOU'LL HAVE SPIDER-MAN'S HEAD ON YOUR WALL.

...NO PRESENTS.

HAPPY BIRTHDAY, AUNT MAY!

PETER PARKER, I *TOLD* YOU...

I KNOW. BUT MY HOMEMADE CAKE IS PRETTY MUCH A DISASTER.

PLUS, THIS WAS JUST SOMETHING I FOUND.

REMEMBER MY FIRST NIGHT HERE? I COULDN'T SLEEP IN MY ROOM, SO--

YOUR UNCLE BEN AND I CAMPED OUT WITH YOU. WE BUILT A LITTLE PILLOW FORT AND USED BEN'S CAMERA FLASH FOR--

OH, PETER...

FORT PARKER

...IT'S PERFECT.

HAPPY BIRTHDAY, AUNT MAY.

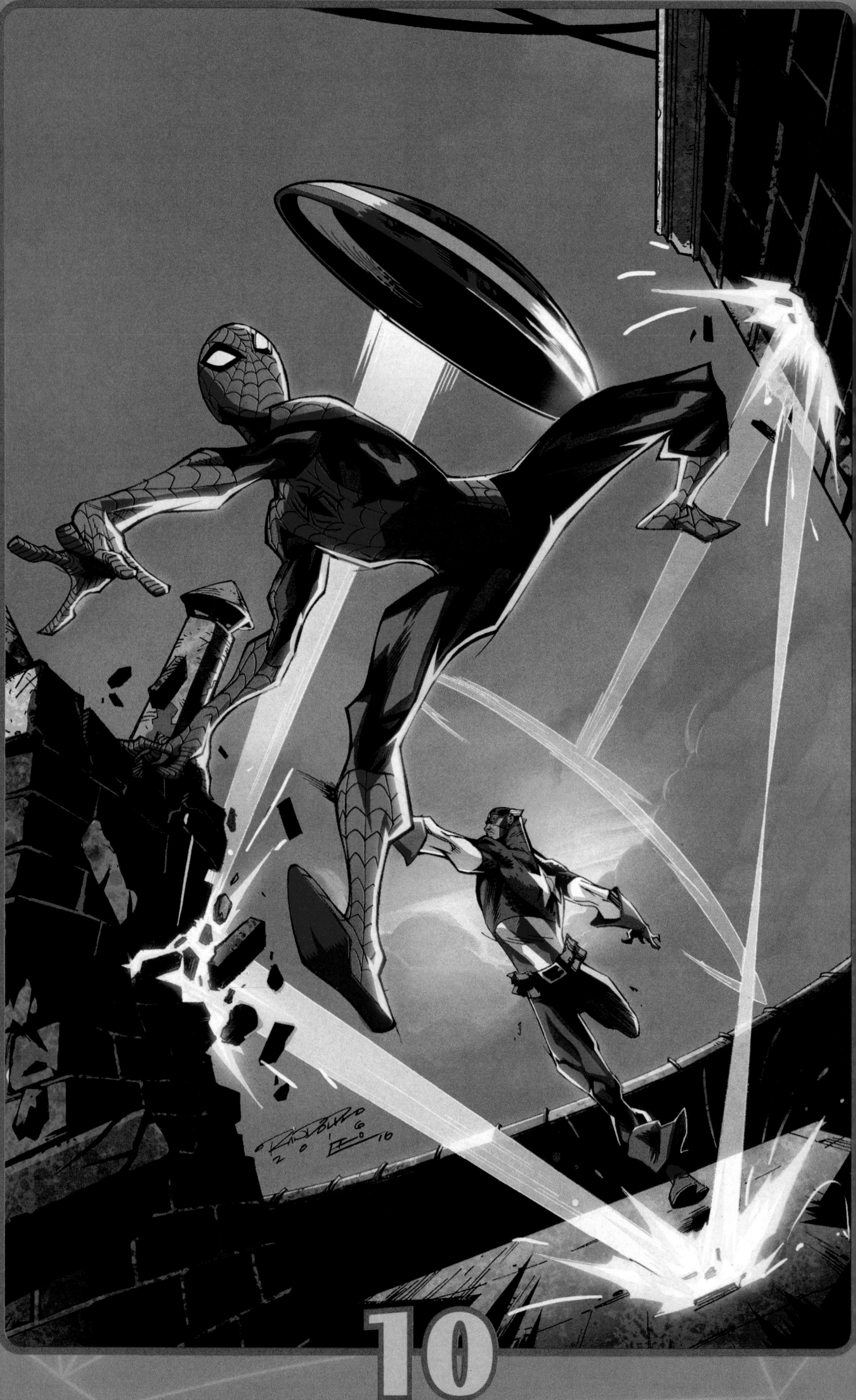

10

HSSSS!!

I LOVE YOU, TOO, MR. MITTENS.

BEING A HERO. THE GLAMOROUS LIFE, RIGHT?

BUT, HEY, PEOPLE *LOVE* ME.

HERE YOU GO, LITTLE GUY--

MOMMY! THE SPIDER-THING HAS MR. MITTENS!

I MEAN, *SOME* PEOPLE LOVE ME.

NO, I WOULD NEVER TAKE A CAT. BESIDES, I'M MORE OF A DOG PERSON--

HELP! THE SPIDER-THING WANTS TO TAKE OUR DOGS!

OH, WHO AM I KIDDING...

DAILY BUGLE

New York's Finest Daily Newspaper

SPIDER-MAN AND ROBOT TERRORIZE CITY

...NOBODY LOVES ME...

ME

WHAT GOBLIN DOESN'
SPIDEY LOVE?

THRE

SPIDER-MAN BUILDING SPIDER-ARMY

PEST

CRIMIN

NACE!

Editorial by
J. Jonah Jameson

COURGE!

SPIDER-MAN IN
KANGAROO'S POUCH

PLAGUE

THE REAL KINGPIN?

NUISANCE

BAD
REPUTATION

ROBBIE
THOMPSON
writer

NATHAN
STOCKMAN
artist

JIM
CAMPBELL
colors

VC's TRAVIS LANHAM lettering
KHARY RANDOLPH & EMILIO LOPEZ cover

DARREN SHAN editor NICK LOWE executive editor
AXEL ALONSO editor in chief JOE QUESADA chief creative officer
DAN BUCKLEY publisher ALAN FINE executive producer

SPIDER-MAN created by STAN LEE & STEVE DITKO

AL!

...BUT...I'M WORKING ON MY REPUTATION.

WHO ARE YOU TALKING TO?

STEP ONE: DON'T SAY THOUGHTS OUT LOUD.

I'M CALLING THE POLICE!

GREAT, MAYBE YOU CAN TELL THEM I--

YOU'LL BE UNDER ARREST SOON ENOUGH, YOU PIECE OF--

‡SIGH‡

MAYBE I NEED TO HIRE A P.R. PERSON?

OR MAYBE JUST SHOUT IT FROM THE ROOFTOPS?

MY NAME IS SPIDER-MAN AND I'M HERE TO HELP!

IS THAT SO?

CAPTAIN AMERICA?!

THAT'S WHAT IT SAYS ON THE BACK OF THE SHIELD.

WOW. UM, HI? I'M, UH, I'M SPIDER-MAN.

WITH A HYPHEN. SO I'VE HEARD.

WAIT, HE'S HEARD OF ME? OH MAN, IT'S PROBABLY ALL BAD STUFF.

C'MON, PETER, DON'T BLOW THIS--BE COOL, FOR ONCE IN YOUR SAD LITTLE LIFE! BE REMOTELY COOL!

YOU'VE HEARD OF ME?! I MEAN. YOU HAVE. I HAVE HEARD OF YOU ALSO AS WELL, TOO.

I. AM. THE. WORST.

THIS IS MY NEIGHBORHOOD.

I'M JUST OUT FOR A PATROL.

MAYBE YOU'D CARE TO JOIN ME?

UM... SURE?

I MEAN...YES. PLEASE.

C'MON, SPIDER-MAN.

LET'S GO DO SOME GOOD.

SO, HERE ARE SOME FUN FACTS ABOUT CAPTAIN AMERICA.

HE IS A SUPER-SOLDIER.

PRODUCT OF GOVERNMENT EXPERIMENTS.

HE FOUGHT IN WORLD WAR II. PUNCHED HITLER IN THE NECK.

THEN GOT FROZEN FOR DECADES.

THAWED OUT IN MODERN TIMES.

HE'S POWERED BY A SUPER-SOLDIER SERUM.

BEFORE THAT? HE WAS A LITTLE GEEK...

...JUST LIKE *ME*.

UN-LIKE ME?

PEOPLE *LOVE* THIS GUY.

IS THERE A FREEZER NEARBY?

MAYBE I CAN GET FROZEN...

...THEN THAWED OUT IN THIRTY YEARS WHEN PEOPLE ARE READY TO LOVE A SPIDER-THEMED HERO.

CAN I ASK YOU SOMETHING?

HE SPEAKS! TO ME, NO LESS!

UH, SURE?

REALLY GOTTA WORK ON ANSWERING QUESTIONS WITHOUT AN ADDED QUESTION MARK ON THE END.

WHY DO YOU DO THIS?

RESPECTFULLY, YOU'RE JUST A KID.

YOU SHOULD BE OUT THERE DOING KID THINGS.

"I DO IT FOR THE LOVE, CAP--"

"I DO IT FOR AMERICA, CAP--"

NO. C'MON, PARKER. THIS IS CAP. BE SERIOUS.

A LONG TIME AGO...SOMEONE TOLD ME THAT WITH GREAT POWER, THERE MUST ALSO COME GREAT RESPONSIBILITY.

I CAN HELP. SO I DO HELP. TRY TO, ANYWAY.

GOOD ANSWER.

CAN I ASK YOU SOMETHING?

SURE.

YOU KNOW WHAT? HOLD THAT THOUGHT--

ZZZAMMM

FRIENDS OF YOURS?

YEAH, WE GO BACK.

UM, OKAY, DO YOU WANT TO TAKE OUT THE TEN GUYS ON THE LEFT, AND I'LL TAKE OUT THE TWO ON THE RIGHT, OR--

FIRST THING TO DO IN A SITUATION LIKE THIS?

DON'T PANIC.

I'M TOTALLY PANICKING.

NO PROBLEM. NOT PANICKING. AT ALL.

TODAY, YOU SHALL PAY...

SECOND THING, DON'T ENGAGE IN SMALL TALK WITH THE SMALL-MINDED.

TOTALLY. WHO HAS TWO THUMBS AND DOESN'T TALK TO BAD GUYS MID-FIGHT? NOT THIS GUY.

DON'T QUIP, DON'T QUIP, DON'T QUIP, DON'T QUIP.

DEATH TO CAPTAIN AMERICA!

I'VE *BEEN* DEAD. DIDN'T REALLY WORK FOR ME.

MAN, WHAT *HAVEN'T* YOU DONE?

A CROSSWORD PUZZLE.

YEAH, ME, NEITHER. WHICH IS WEIRD 'CAUSE I LOVE SCRABBLE.

NOT REALLY, ONE'S A WORD GAME, THE OTHER A NUMBERS GAME.

TOUCHÉ.

OKAY, WHAT GIVES? WHY THE ATTACK?

WE WERE JUST THE OPENING ACT.

UH, CAP, I THINK THE MAIN ATTRACTION JUST ARRIVED...

ANY CHANCE YOU'VE EVER FOUGHT A GIANT FLOATING HEAD WITH ITTY-BITTY ARMS?

I SHOULD HAVE KNOWN. WHERE THERE'S A.I.M....

...THERE'S **M.O.D.O.K.!**

FEEL THE WRATH OF MY MENTAL BOLTS!

FWASSSH

THWIP

KSSH

OOOF!

SMART THINKING, KID.

YOU HAVE BEEN A THORN IN A.I.M.'S SIDE FOR TOO LONG, CAPTAIN. THAT ENDS TODAY. YOU END TODAY!

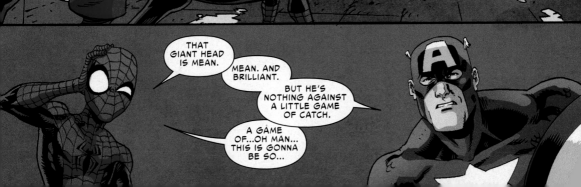

THAT GIANT HEAD IS MEAN.

MEAN. AND BRILLIANT. BUT HE'S NOTHING AGAINST A LITTLE GAME OF CATCH.

A GAME OF...OH MAN... THIS IS GONNA BE SO...

"...AWESOME!"

HIS NAME IS SPIDER-MAN AND YOU...

NO! YOU SHALL NOT VANQUISH ME, CAPTAIN AMERICA! NOT YOU, OR YOUR LITTLE FRIEND!

...ARE DONE FOR THE NIGHT!

AAAAGH!

ALL RIGHT, SPIDER-MAN, LET'S TAKE CARE OF--

WOW.

NOT BAD, KID. NOT BAD AT ALL.

I LEARNED IT FROM WATCHING YOU.

I MEAN, EXCEPT THE WEB PARTS. THAT WAS ALL ME.

YOU DID WELL TODAY. KEEP UP THE GOOD WORK.

AND STAY IN SCHOOL.

YESSIR.

HEY... WHAT WERE YOU GONNA ASK ME BEFORE?

I WAS GONNA ASK...WHY DO PEOPLE LOVE YOU SO MUCH?

BUT TO BE HONEST? HAVING A FRONT ROW SEAT TODAY SHOWED ME WHY.

REPUTATIONS COME AND GO. SOMETIMES YOU'RE A GOOD GUY. SOMETIMES YOU'RE A BAD GUY.

ALL THAT MATTERS IS WHAT YOU DO NEXT.

HE'S RIGHT.

HE'S CAPTAIN AMERICA.

HE'S ALWAYS RIGHT.

SO... HOW'D THE KID DO?

IRON MAN'S ASSESSMENT WAS SPOT-ON. HE'S GETTING THERE, COULSON.

YOU LIKE HIM, THEN?

WHO DOESN'T?

THE NEXT DAY...

?

DAILY BUGLE

New York's Finest Daily Newspaper

SPIDER-MAN, AGENT OF A.I.M.?

Webbed menace seen training with A.I.M. soldiers

Editorial by J. Jonah Jameson

"I'M SORRY, MR. JAMESON, BUT--"

"I SAID NO CALLS OR MEETINGS, MS. BRANT! WHAT COULD POSSIBLY--"

--OH, *UH*, HELLO, MISTER, I MEAN, CAPTAIN--

MR. JAMESON. I'D LIKE TO TALK TO YOU ABOUT THIS HEADLINE.

WHAT, *UH*, WHAT ABOUT--

I WAS *WITH* SPIDER-MAN YESTERDAY. WE TOOK DOWN M.O.D.O.K. AND AN A.I.M. CELL...

...TOGETHER.

HE'S NOT A MENACE.

I KNOW WHAT A *MENACE* LOOKS LIKE.

SO... WHY DON'T YOU GRAB A PENCIL...

DAILY BUGLE

New York's Finest Daily Newspaper

CAPTAIN AMERICA AND SPIDER-MAN SAVE CITY FROM M.O.D.O.K.

"Spider-Man is an asset to New York"

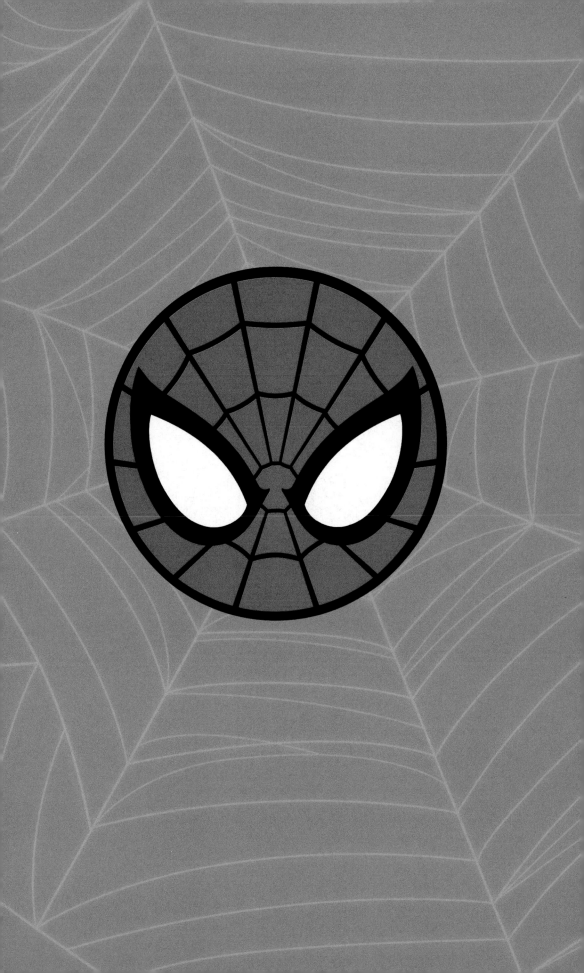

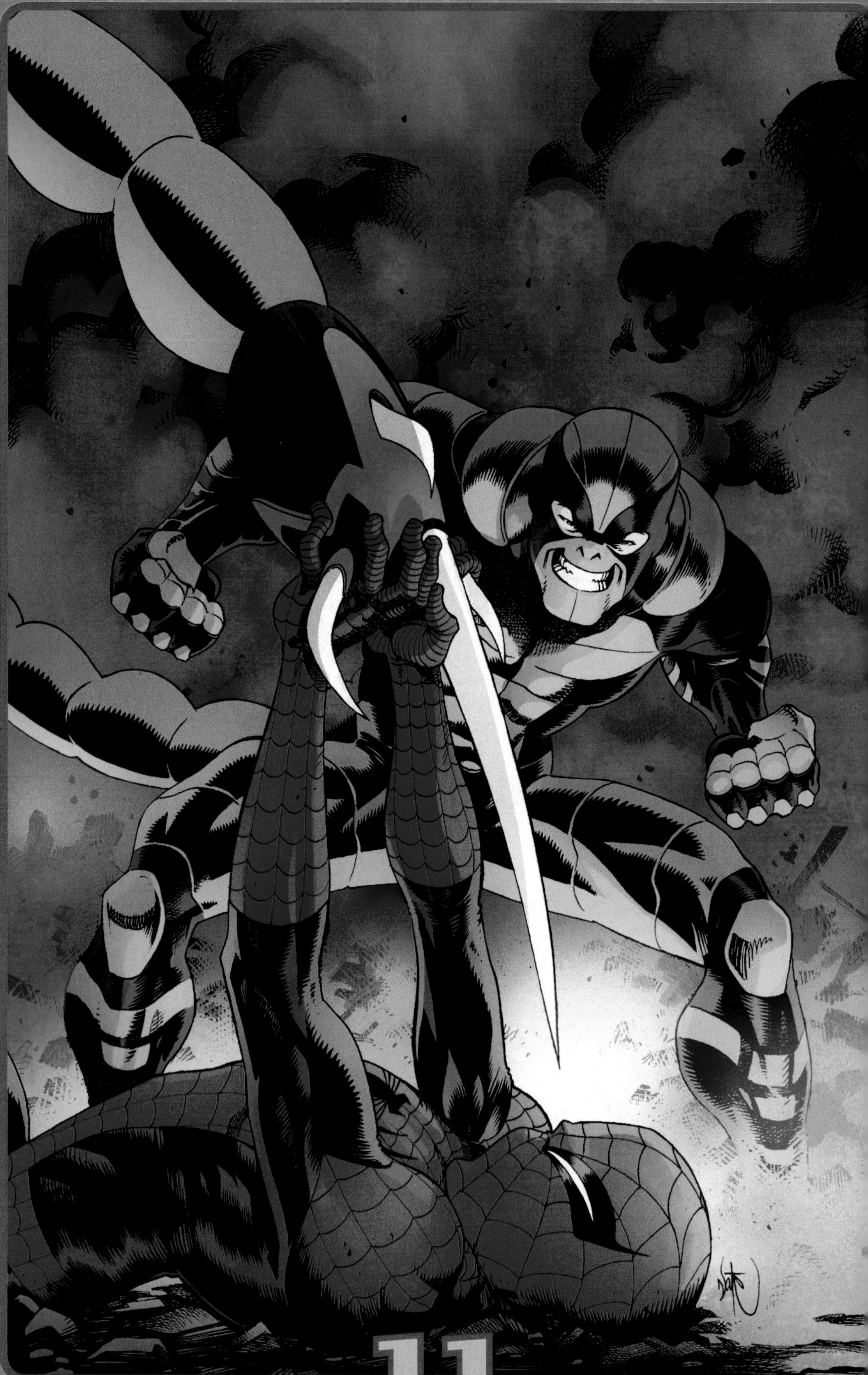

11

REMEMBER CINDY

ALL RIGHT, TEAM PARKER, HERE WE GO.

SOME CAFFEINE TO POWER US THROUGH.

UH, YEAH, I'M GOOD, THANKS.

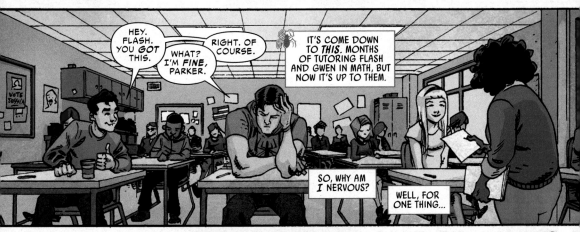

HEY. FLASH. YOU *GOT* THIS.

WHAT? I'M *FINE*, PARKER.

RIGHT. OF COURSE.

IT'S COME DOWN TO *THIS*. MONTHS OF TUTORING FLASH AND GWEN IN MATH, BUT NOW IT'S UP TO THEM.

SO, WHY AM *I* NERVOUS?

WELL, FOR ONE THING...

...I MAY, OR MAY NOT, HAVE AN ENORMOUS CRUSH ON GWEN STACY.

BEING HER TUTOR, I'VE DISCOVERED SHE'S EVEN SMARTER AND MORE AWESOME THAN I THOUGHT. HAVE I MENTIONED SHE'S FUNNY, TOO?

AS FOR MY *OTHER* TUTEE...

=SIGH=

...IF *FLASH THOMPSON* FAILS...

...HE RETURNS TO HIS BULLYING WAYS.

SO, YEAH. *THAT'S* WHY I'M NERVOUS.

BRRRNNG

PENCILS DOWN, GANG.

SO?

I...I ACTUALLY THINK...I THINK I DID OKAY.

I GUESS PARKER'S GOOD FOR *SOMETHING.*

I *KNEW* YOU COULD DO IT!

AND PETER'S THE *BEST.*

WAIT. DID SHE SAY "BEST"? IN REFERENCE TO ME?

LET'S HEAD TO LEO'S TO CELEBRATE!

TABLE FOR THREE-- BURGERS ON ME!

RIGHT... TABLE FOR THREE...

WAIT... WHAT'S--

BUMP

I KNOW. I KNOW.

I COULD HAVE CAUGHT IT. BUT USING MY SUPER REFLEXES WITHOUT A MASK ON? BAD IDEA FOR THE OL' SECRET IDENTITY.

AND *THAT'S* WHY WE DON'T ALLOW DRINKS IN CLASS, MR. PARKER.

BUT IT WASN'T...I DIDN'T--

ACCIDENTS HAPPEN.

YEAH, THEY SURE DO.

DON'T WORRY. WE'LL SAVE YOU A SEAT, PARKER.

YOU CAN STAY AFTER AND COPY YOUR RESULTS INTO SOMETHING A BIT LESS DAMP.

REMEMBER CINDY

I'M GLAD TO SEE FLASH GETTING SOME HELP FROM YOU, PETER. HE DESERVES A BREAK.

YEAH, A BREAK IN HIS STUPID--WAIT, *WHAT?*

HOW DO YOU MEAN?

YOU + THE SUN!

NOT EVERYONE HAS SOMEONE KIND LIKE YOUR AUNT MAY TO LOOK AFTER THEM, MR. PARKER.

WHAT DOES *THAT* MEAN?

AND HOW DOES THAT EXCUSE FLASH FROM BEING A JERK?

=SIGH= WELL, I GUESS ONCE AGAIN, I'M...

MISSING OUT

GWEN AND FLASH WERE GONE BY THE TIME I GOT THERE, OF COURSE.

THAT'S FINE. I HAVE THINGS TO DO, TOO.

DON'T WORRY, I GOT YOU.

IS THIS REAL LIFE?

PROBABLY.

WALK-UPS ARE THE WORST, RIGHT?

DO YOU ALWAYS WEAR THAT OUTFIT?

ONLY WHEN I'M TRYING TO IMPRESS PEOPLE.

GOOD LUCK WITH THAT.

THIS IS A SPIDER-BANDAGE. IT WILL HEAL YOU TWICE AS FAST.

YOU'RE NOT WRONG, KID.

YOU'RE WEIRD.

SO, YEAH. FINE. I MISSED OUT ON HANGING WITH GWEN. I'M SURE SHE AND FLASH HAD A GREAT TIME.

IT'S COOL. I'VE GOT A LOT GOING ON, TOO.

NONE OF WHICH INVOLVES GWEN.

I'VE WASTED MY LIFE.

WHAT THE--

HOLY AWESOME!

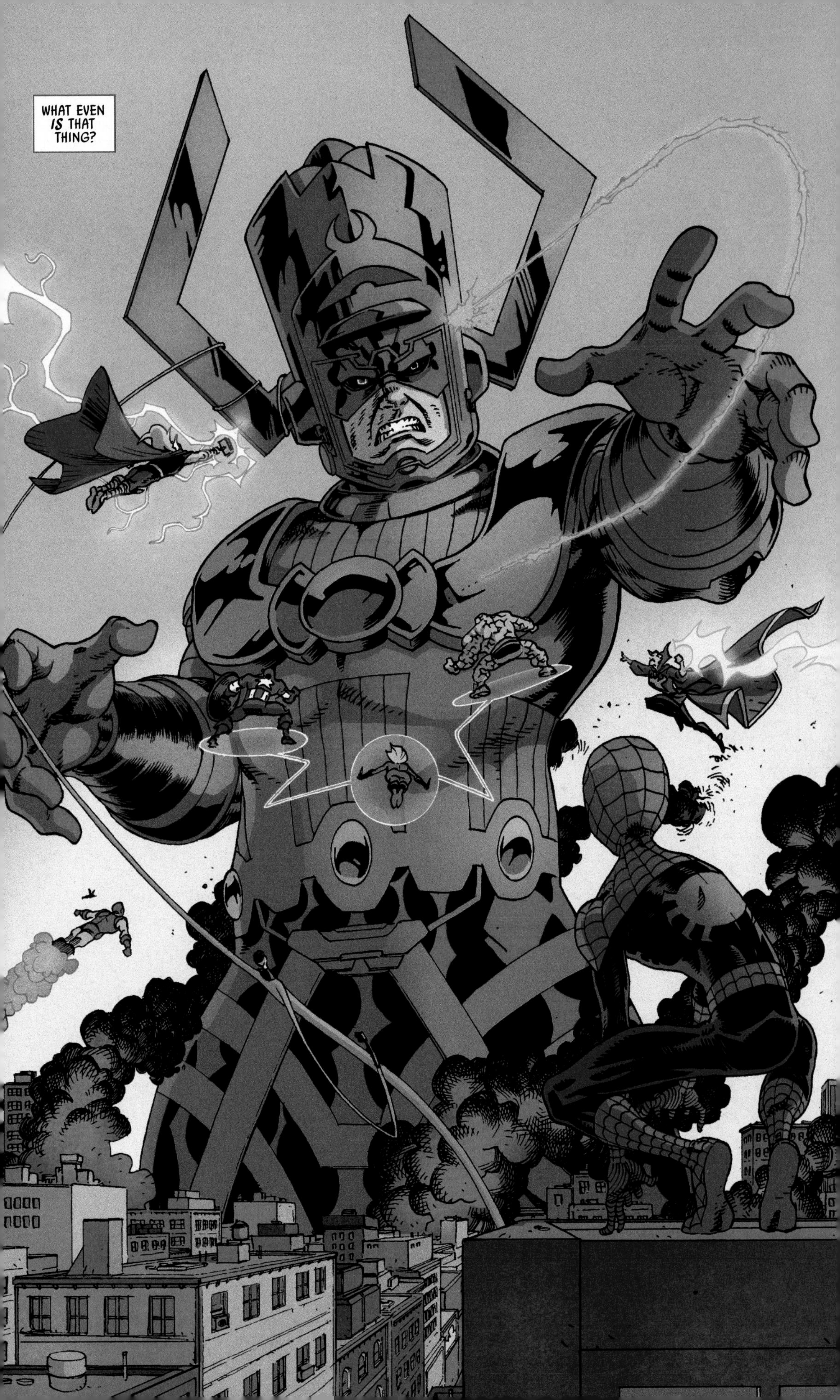
WHAT EVEN *IS* THAT THING?

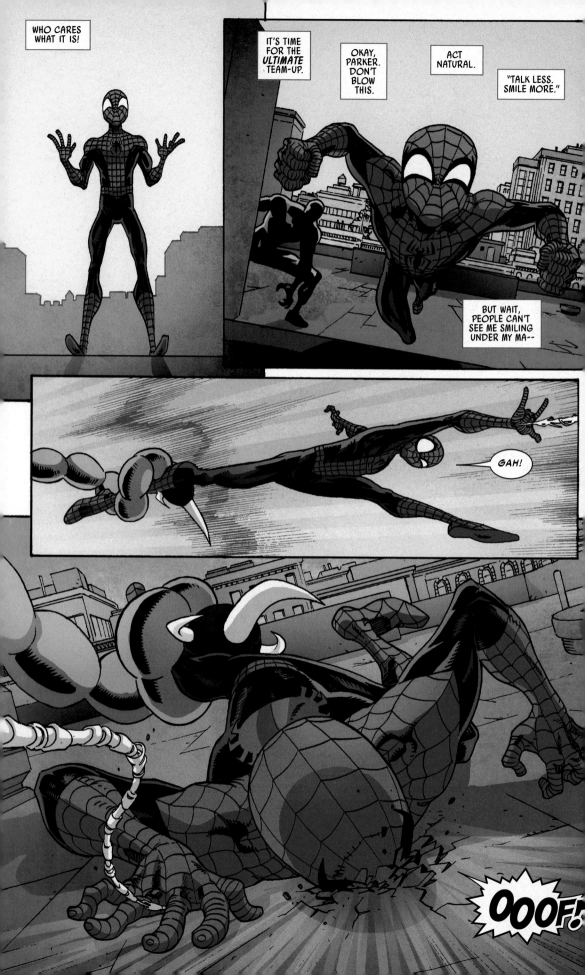

WHO CARES WHAT IT IS!

IT'S TIME FOR THE ULTIMATE TEAM-UP.

OKAY, PARKER. DON'T BLOW THIS.

ACT NATURAL.

"TALK LESS. SMILE MORE."

BUT WAIT, PEOPLE CAN'T SEE ME SMILING UNDER MY MA--

GAH!

OOOF!

TONIGHT, YOU DIE!

UM, NO THANK YOU?

GREAT. JUST WHAT I NEEDED.

SCORPION.

I DON'T KNOW IF YOU CAN SEE THROUGH ALL THAT GREEN, BUT THERE'S A GIANT DESTROYING THE WEST VILLAGE.

CAN YOU ATTEMPT TO MURDER ME ANOTHER NIGHT?

GRAWWWL!!

I HEAR YOU. I DO. BUT I DON'T HAVE TIME FOR YOU RIGHT NOW.

SOMETHING'S OFF WITH SCORPION. HE'S USUALLY MORE CHATTY THAN THIS.

IS IT ME? SOMETHING I SAID?

YOU... DIE...

UM, ME... LIVE...?

I'LL LET S.H.I.E.L.D. FIGURE THIS OUT.

THEY DO PICK-UP SERVICE, RIGHT?

WHAT'S 9-1-1 FOR S.H.I.E.L.D. AGAIN?

AAGH!

WELL, THAT'S NEW.

SERIOUSLY, WHAT'S UP WITH THIS DUDE?

YOU... YOU MUST DIE...

YOU KEEP SAYING THAT. I DON'T THINK IT'S GONNA CATCH ON.

THE... THE *VOICES* SAY SO...

YOU HAVE VOICES IN YOUR HEAD TOO?

DO THEY SING ABBA? 'CAUSE MINE ARE ALWAYS BUSTING OUT "DANCING QUEE--"

OOOF!

SHOULDN'T WE BE MULTI-LEGGED TOTEM BROS?

OOF!

VOICES IN HIS HEAD. YEAH, *SOMETHING'S* CHANGED SINCE I LAST DANCED WITH OL' SCORPORINO.

HIS *REAL* NAME IS MAC GARGAN.

GOT BONDED WITH THE STRENGTH AND POWER OF AN ACTUAL SCORPION.

NOT EXACTLY MY BIGGEST FAN.

HA. LIKE I HAVE *ANY* FANS.

OKAY, SCORPORINO, THIS HAS BEEN FUN, BUT LIKE I SAID...

VERTICAL STRIPES, THOUGH. MORE SLIMMING.

IS THIS 'CAUSE I DON'T HAVE A TAIL?

I COULD *TRY* ONE, MAYBE SOMETHING WITH STRIPES?

...I GOT *PLANS* TONIGHT.

AND FOR ONCE? I AM *NOT* MISSING OUT ON THE FUN.

OKAY, TELL YOU WHAT WE'LL DO.

YOU HANG HERE FOR A BIT WHILE I GO AFTER THE PURPLE PEOPLE EATER OVER THERE.

AND WE'LL CONTINUE THIS CONVERSATION WHEN I GET BACK.

RRIIIP

REALLY?

DO ME A SOLID AND DON'T TURN THE PAGE.

YOU JUST *HAD* TO DO IT, DIDN'T YOU?

VOICES... SAY...YOU...

...DIE!

KRNCH

LET'S TRY THIS AGAIN.

I'VE ENJOYED OUR TIME TOGETHER.

ESPECIALLY THE PART WHERE YOU KEEP SAYING THE SAME THING OVER AND OVER AGAIN.

BUT I *REALLY* HAVE TO GO.

MAN, I LOVE NEW YORK!

GET 'IM, GREEN TAIL GUY!

QUIET DOWN! PEOPLE ARE TRYING TO WATCH NETFLIX!

KRNCH

TOUCHDOWN!

SORRY.

GAH! I SAID I WAS SORRY!

Y'KNOW WHAT?

TAILS ARE OUT THIS YEAR.

NO!

YES! THE...THE VOICES...

YEAH, I KNOW--

...PLEASE...

...PLEASE GET THEM OUT OF MY HEAD...

WAIT... WHAT?

UM, WAS THIS METAL THING ALWAYS THERE?

AAAGH!

THANK... THANK YOU...

WHAT THE--

PERFECT. IT SELF-DESTRUCTED.

NOTHING OMINOUS ABOUT THAT.

NOPE. NOT EVEN A LITTLE BIT.

I...I WOKE UP IN THE SUIT...

I'M SORRY, I--I DIDN'T WANT THIS.

I'D BEEN GOOD. I'VE BEEN SEEING THE DOCS AND--

HEY. THIS WASN'T YOUR FAULT.

RIIIP

SOMEONE USED *YOU* TO TRY TO GET TO *ME*.

I GUESS IT'S BACK TO JAIL, HUH?

FORTUNATELY FOR YOU...I'VE GOT BIGGER FISH TO FRY.

STARTING WITH THE GIANT PURPLE DUDE...

...AND ENDING WITH FIGURING OUT WHO SENT A SCORPION TO KILL A SPIDER...

I TOLD YOU SCORPION WOULD BE A FAILURE.

NO MATTER...

...SIX IS A MUCH BETTER NUMBER.

MUST SWING FASTER. MUST SWING--

HELP!

HEY, I THINK YOU DROPPED THIS.

FOR YOUR TROUBLE, YOUNG MAN.

NO THANKS, MA'AM-- ACTION IS MY REWARD!

HOW RUDE.

OKAY, FELLOW HEROES, THE CAVALRY HAS--

OH, COME ON.

BUT... I'M HERE... TO HELP...

YA CAN HELP BY CLEANIN' UP THIS MESS, WEB-HEAD.

⇥SIGH⇤

CLEAN UP, AISLE THREE.

ANYONE? ANYONE?

⇥SIGH⇤

MAYBE *TODAY* WILL BE DIFFERENT. MAYBE --

MIDTOWN HIGH SCHOOL

DAD, LISTEN, I--

NO. *YOU* LISTEN.

YOU SHUT UP. AND LISTEN TO ME.

UNDERSTAND?

YOUR GRADES ARE IN THE TOILET. *YOU'RE* IN THE TOILET.

NOW GET INSIDE THERE AND DO SOMETHING SMART FOR ONCE IN YOUR *STUPID* LIFE.

YESSIR.

SO *THAT'S* WHAT MRS. EASTMAN MEANT.

OH, *UH,* HEY PARKER.

C'MON, PETER. LET HIM OFF THE HOOK.

DID YOU, *UH,* WALK TO SCHOOL TODAY?

UM, YEAH. YEAH, I DID.

BIG DAY TODAY. TESTS COME BACK.

YEAH. YEAH, THEY DO. I REALLY NEED TO PASS THAT--

I KNOW, FLASH. DON'T WORRY. WE GOT THIS.

I DID IT!

WE DID IT!

THANKS, PARKER.

I GOT AN A. AN A!

WOW, THAT'S GREAT!

BUT YOU GUYS DID THE WORK.

COURSE. SEE YOU GUYS AT LEO'S.

PETER, THESE PAST COUPLE OF MONTHS, IT'S BEEN GREAT GETTING TO HANG OUT, BUT NOW THAT THE TEST IS OVER, WELL, I WAS TALKING TO FLASH AND--

NOPE. TODAY WILL NOT BE DIFFERENT.

OH. OH, I GET IT. I DO. I'LL SEE YOU AROUND.

NO, PETER. I... WHAT I'M TRYING TO SAY IS...

...WILL YOU GO TO THE DANCE WITH ME?

WELL, TODAY IS A NEW DAY AFTER ALL.

SO MUCH FOR MISSING OUT...

HOMECOMING DANCE OCT 12 SAVE THE DATE!

VOTE LIZ FOR HC QUEEN!

GUITAR LESSONS

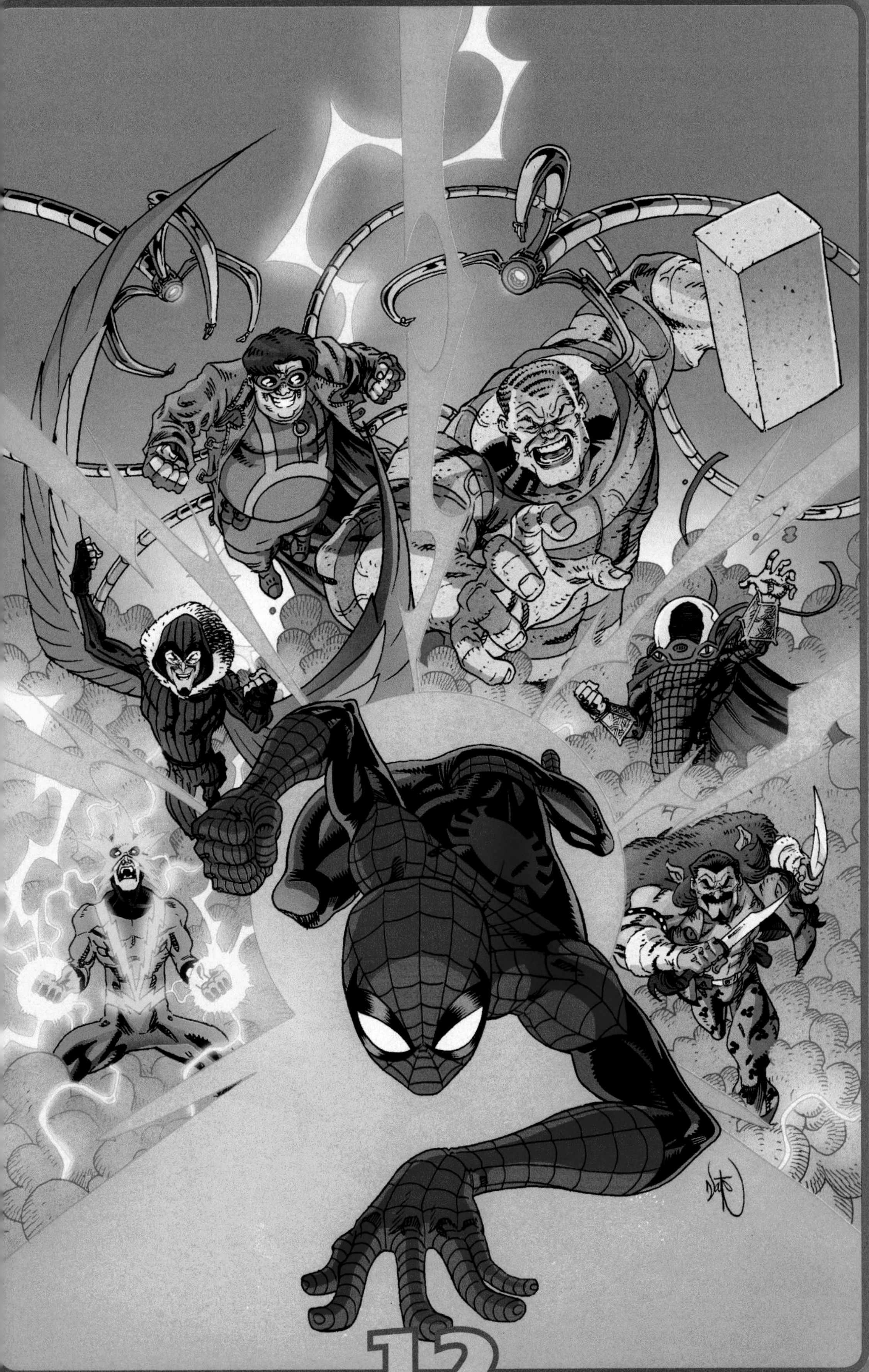

12

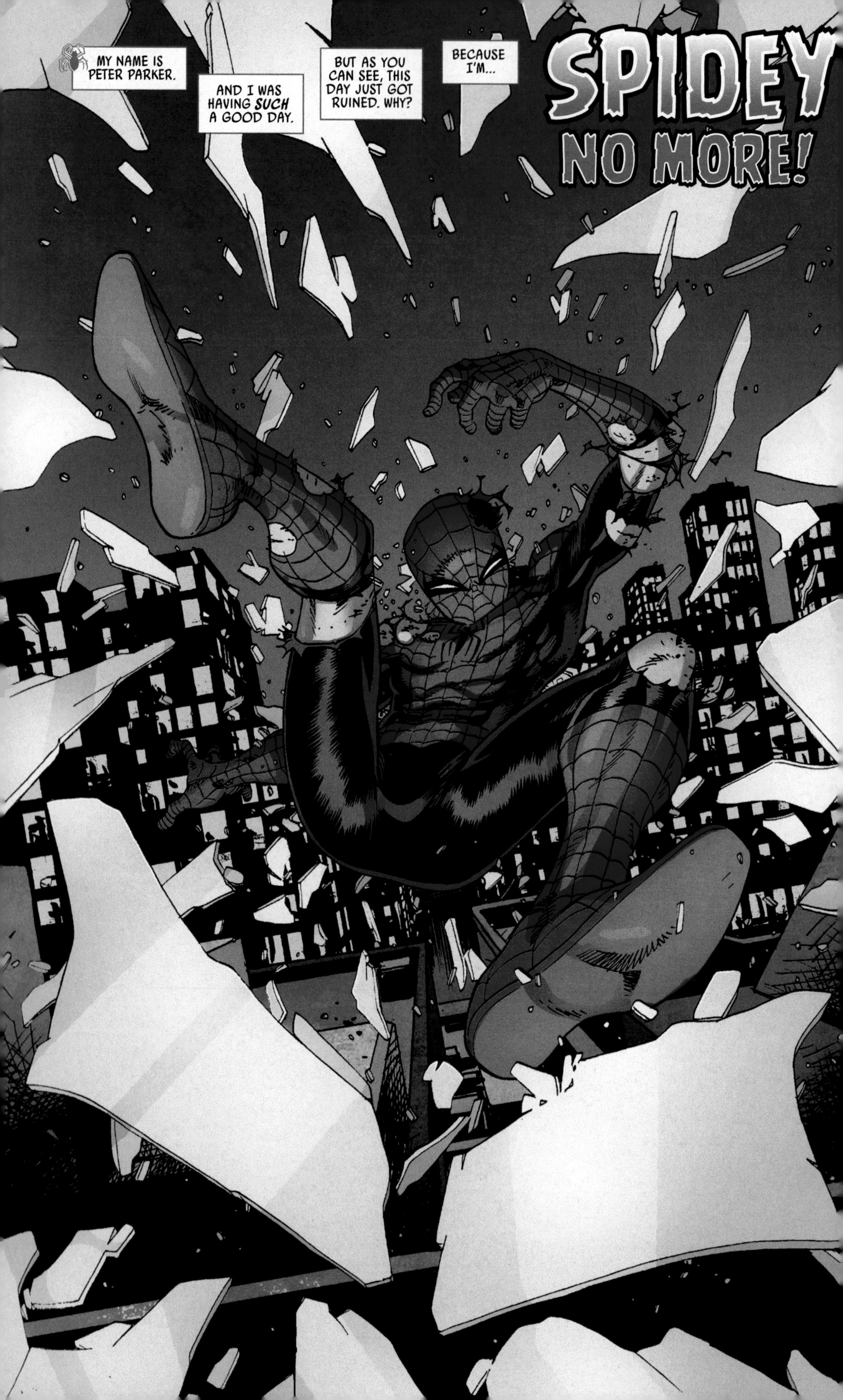

MY NAME IS PETER PARKER.
AND I WAS HAVING SUCH A GOOD DAY.
BUT AS YOU CAN SEE, THIS DAY JUST GOT RUINED. WHY?
BECAUSE I'M...
SPIDEY NO MORE!

PARKER RESIDENCE. EARLIER.

AUNT MAY, WHERE ARE YOU OFF TO?

I DIDN'T WANT TO SAY ANYTHING UNTIL IT WAS FOR SURE, BUT NO MORE UNEMPLOYMENT FOR YOUR OLD AUNT MAY...

...I FOUND A JOB. I'LL BE WORKING AT THE SHELTER FULL-TIME NOW. PAID, NO LESS!

OH WOW, AUNT MAY, THAT'S GREAT!

I'M SORRY I WON'T BE ABLE TO SEE YOU OFF FOR THE BIG NIGHT.

TAKE LOTS OF PICTURES!

I ALWAYS DO!

SEE? TOLD YOU. GOOD. DAY.

AND IT GOT EVEN BETTER.

WELL, WHAT DO YOU KNOW, PARKER?

YOU *FINALLY* TOOK SOME PICTURES THAT WEREN'T *AWFUL.*

I'LL TAKE THESE TWO. THE REST ARE GARBAGE, AS USUAL.

UM, MR. JAMESON, IS...IS THERE ANY WAY I COULD GET PAID TODAY--

PAYDAY'S AT THE END OF THE WEEK. NO EXCEPTIONS.

NO... I KNOW. IT'S JUST... I--

SPIT IT OUT, PARKER!

IT'S HOMECOMING AND I NEED MONEY FOR MY TUX AND FOR DINNER AND I KNOW THERE'S NO EXCEPTIONS BUT I HAD TO TRY AND I'M SORRY AND I'LL SEE MYSELF OUT.

J.JONAH JAMESON
EDITOR IN CHIEF

PARKER! SHUT UP AND LISTEN.

SUITS & TUXEDOS

TUXEDO RENTAL FROM $99

SEE? AND THEN, AFTER ALL THIS...

...MY DAY WENT FROM GOOD...

...TO AMAZING.

HAPPY HOMECOMING

LOOKING GOOD, YOU TWO.

LOOKING GOOD YOURSELF, FLASH.

DON'T RUIN THE MOMENT, DUMMY.

I ALMOST *DID* RUIN THE MOMENT. BECAUSE, WELL, Y'KNOW...

...I'M *ME*.

HEY, GWEN... CAN I ASK YOU SOMETHING?

ANYTHING.

WHY ME?

WHY YOU WHAT?

YOU'RE... *AMAZING.* SMART. FUNNY. BOLD. BADASS. AND I'M...WELL, I'M *ME*.

I'M NOT HEARING A QUESTION, MR. PARKER.

WHY'D YOU ASK ME TO THE DANCE, AND NOT, LIKE, WELL, ANYONE ELSE?

WHEN ARE YOU GONNA REALIZE HOW *GREAT* YOU ARE, PETER?

DON'T WORRY. WE KEPT DANCING.

BECAUSE GWEN REALLY IS THE BEST.

AND THEN WE WENT WHERE TEENAGERS GO WHEN THEY RUN OUT OF PLACES TO HANG--

--AN ALL-NIGHT DINER.

OPEN 24 HOURS

YOU TOOK THIS PHOTO?

YEAH. MR. JAMESON ACTUALLY LIKED THIS ONE FOR ONCE, TOO.

HUH. I'VE MET SPIDEY, Y'KNOW. HE LOOKS TALLER IN PERSON.

YEAH, I GET THAT A LOT--

--TOO, I ALSO GET THAT, A LOT, ALSO.

SPIDEY'S PRETTY GREAT, RIGHT? COOL COSTUME. SUPER-DUDE.

HE'S ALL RIGHT, I GUESS. HIS COSTUME COULD USE A LITTLE MORE PIZZAZZ.

REALLY? I THINK IT'S ICONI--

PLUS--

--HE'S NO PETER PARKER.

YUP. SHE SAID THAT.

AND IN THIS EPIC MOMENT?

MY SPIDER-SENSE WENT OFF. PERFECT TIMING.

AND THUS, MY PERFECT DAY CAME TO AN END. WELL, ALMOST...

UH, YEAH. I'M, UH, I'M SURE ME.

LISTEN, GWEN, IT'S PRETTY LATE, AND YOUR DAD'S A COP, SO--

YOU'RE RIGHT, YOU'RE RIGHT. WE SHOULD CALL IT A NIGHT.

THANKS FOR A PERFECT HOMECOMING, GWEN STACY.

AND THANK YOU, PETER PARKER...

...FOR THE PERFECT KISS.

WHA--

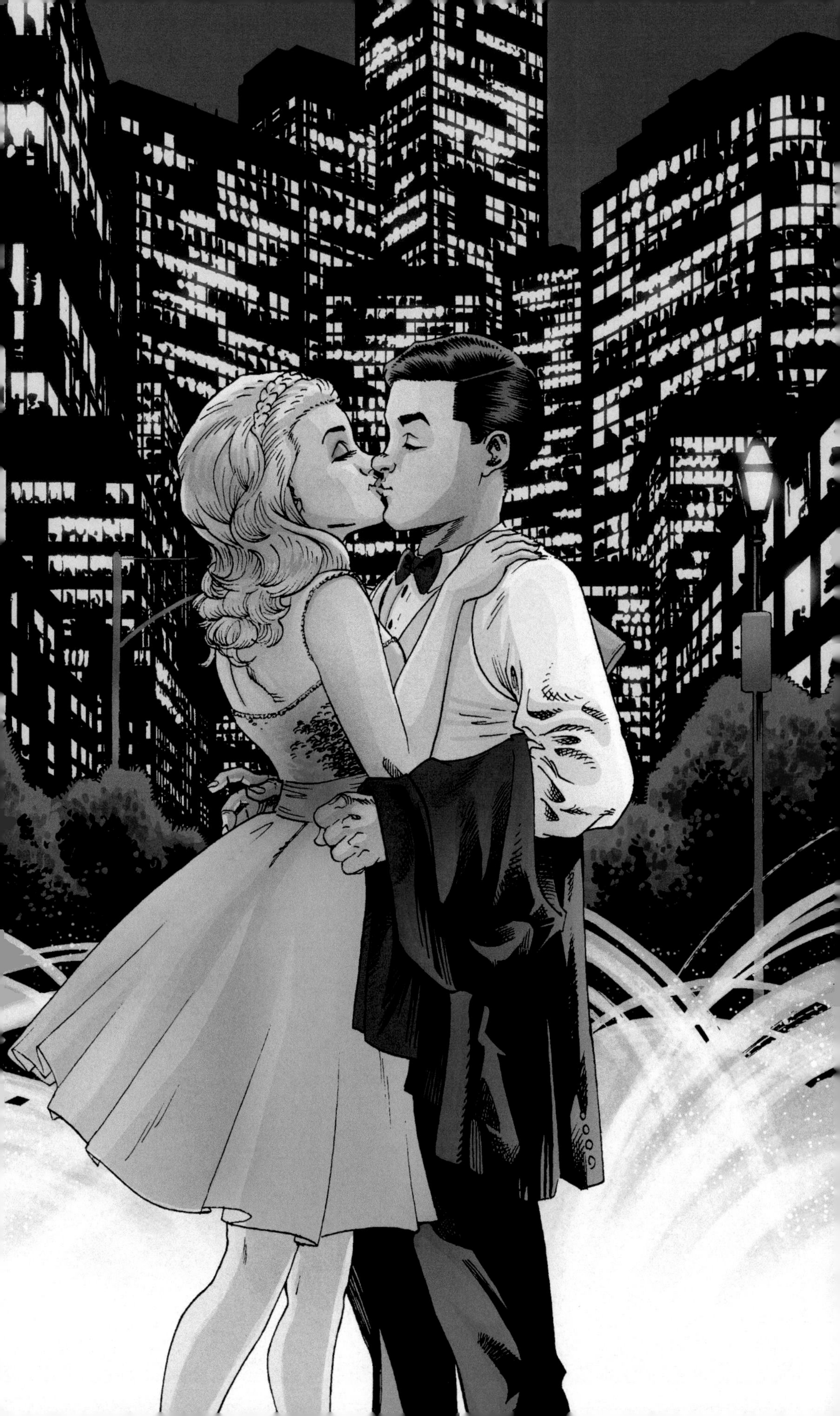

SO, YEAH.

GOOD. AMAZING. PERFECT DAY.

THEN...I JUST HAD TO GO AND RUIN IT.

'CAUSE I'M, WELL, Y'KNOW...ME.

HELP, PLEASE!

BE RIGHT WITH YOU, JUST TRYING NOT TO FREAK OUT INTERNALLY ABOUT WHAT JUST--

Y'KNOW WHAT?

I'LL EXPLAIN LATER.

TO MYSELF. AND MAYBE MY BLOG.

JUST KIDDING, WHO BLOGS ANYMORE?

I'LL JUST TALK TO MYSELF.

HERE, LET ME--

HOLOGRAM. COOL.

IT WAS COOL. HIGH TECH. PRETTY TRICKY.

WHICH MEANT...

MYSTERIO!

IF IT ISN'T MY FAVORITE CRYSTAL BALL.

I'VE MISSED YOU, SPIDER.

WE'VE ALL MISSED YOU.

WE'VE ALL MISSED YOU.

WE'VE ALL MISSED YOU.

IS IT BRING YOUR CLONE TO WORK DAY? WHY DOESN'T ANYBODY TELL ME THESE THINGS?

OKAY, ALL OF YOU STAND STILL AND WAIT TO BE PUNCHED, DEAL?

HE DIDN'T MEAN ALL THE HOLOGRAM MYSTERIOS HAD MISSED ME, OF COURSE. I'M NEVER THAT LUCKY. NO, HE MEANT OTHER JERKS LIKE HIM MISSED ME. JERKS LIKE--

--ELECTRO!

BUT I *HAVE* MISSED WATCHING YOU SQUIRM.

ACTUALLY, I DIDN'T MISS YOU AT ALL.

HOW SWEET.

LOOK AT YOU TWO, TEAMING UP LIKE A BUNCH OF GOOD GUYS. AND ALL FOR ME?

THING IS, I'M HAVING KIND OF A GOOD, AMAZING, PERFECT DAY, AND I DON'T THINK I WANT TO RUIN IT WITH--

GAH!

MIND IF I CUT IN, BOYS?

OOOF!

VULTURE. PERFECT.

DOES IT REALLY TAKE *THREE* BAD GUYS TO TAKE ON LITTLE OLD ME?

IT TAKES--

--AS MANY--

--AS NEEDED!

AAAAAND WE'RE BACK.

AND I'M FALLING.

HOPEFULLY THERE'S SOMETHING SOFT FOR ME TO LAND ON BELOW, BECAUSE I'M FEELING SEMI-CONSCIOUS RIGHT NOW.

NICE! AT LAST, MY LUCK HAS CHANGED.

WAIT A SEC...

SIGH.

I JUST *HAD* TO ASK FOR A SOFT LANDING.

YOU'RE *DEAD*, SPIDER.

HOW ABOUT WE JUST MAKE SOME SAND CASTLES? BRAID EACH OTHER'S HAIR--

SANDALS! IT'S BEEN TOO LONG.

SAME DUMB JOKES.

AND I STILL AIN'T LAUGHIN'.

SLAM

HEY, WHERE YA GOIN', SANDALS? I WAS JUST GETTING WARMED UP.

I GOT MY TURN. NOW HE'S UP TO BAT.

HE WHO?

OH, COME ON--

AT LAST. MY HUNT IS OVER. AT LAST--

--YOU ARE OVER!

FIVE OF YOU GUYS FIGHTING OVER LITTLE OLD ME?

I'M FLATTERED. TRULY.

GRRRAHHH!

NOW THERE'S WHAT I'VE WANTED TO SEE FOR A LONG TIME.

YOU, WHERE YOU BELONG...

...AT MY FEET.

SO THIS IS IT. THE END.

LIFE? NOT FLASHING BEFORE MY EYES.

NOPE. ALL I SEE--

--IS TODAY.

THE GOOD, AMAZING, PERFECT DAY.

MY LAST DAY...

...AND ALL ITS PERFECT MOMENTS.

YOU ASKED ME WHY YOU? I'LL TELL YOU, PETER PARKER. SURE, YOU'RE SMART...

...AND TALENTED...

...AND SWEET...

...BUT MOST OF ALL? NO MATTER WHAT LIFE PUTS IN YOUR WAY? NO MATTER WHAT THE OBSTACLE?

YOU ALWAYS KEEP MOVING FORWARD. USUALLY WITH A DUMB JOKE AT YOUR SIDE, BUT YOU NEVER GIVE UP.

I ADMIRE THAT.

I LOVE THAT.

NEVER GIVE UP.

DUMB JOKES.

YUP...

...SOUNDS LIKE ME.

Y'KNOW, I'VE NEVER UNDERSTOOD WHY WE DON'T GET ALONG, OCK.

CAN'T WE JUST FORM A SCIENCE CLUB INSTEAD OF A FIGHT CLUB?

NO? OKAY, FINE.

AND IT'S NOT THE WHOLE EIGHT-APPENDAGE THING WE'VE GOT GOING ON.

WE BOTH LOVE SCIENCE.

WE BOTH LOVE TEAMING UP WITH LIKE-MINDED PEOPLE.

BUT, I'M SORRY, GUYS...

...THIS AIN'T THE END OF ME.

IT IS, HOWEVER, THE END OF THIS COSTUME. WHERE SHOULD I SEND THE BILL?

OH YEAH: PRISON.

YOU WILL RUE THE DAY, SPIDER!

YEAH, YEAH. I PROBABLY WILL.

BUT NOT TODAY.

DAILY BUGLE

New York's Finest Daily Newspaper

SPIDEY SNARES SINISTER SIX

MY NAME IS PETER PARKER.

I WAS BITTEN BY A RADIOACTIVE SPIDER.

I WAS GIVEN GREAT POWERS.

WHICH MY FAMILY TAUGHT ME TO VIEW AS A GREAT RESPONSIBILITY.

I DON'T ALWAYS WIN.

IN FACT, MORE OFTEN THAN NOT, I LOSE.

BUT I NEVER GIVE UP.

WHY?

MORE PIZZAZZ, HUH?

BECAUSE I'M...

the AMAZING SPIDER-MAN!

THE END!

ANDRÉ LIMA ARAÚJO
SPIDEY 7, PAGES 2-3 ART PROCESS

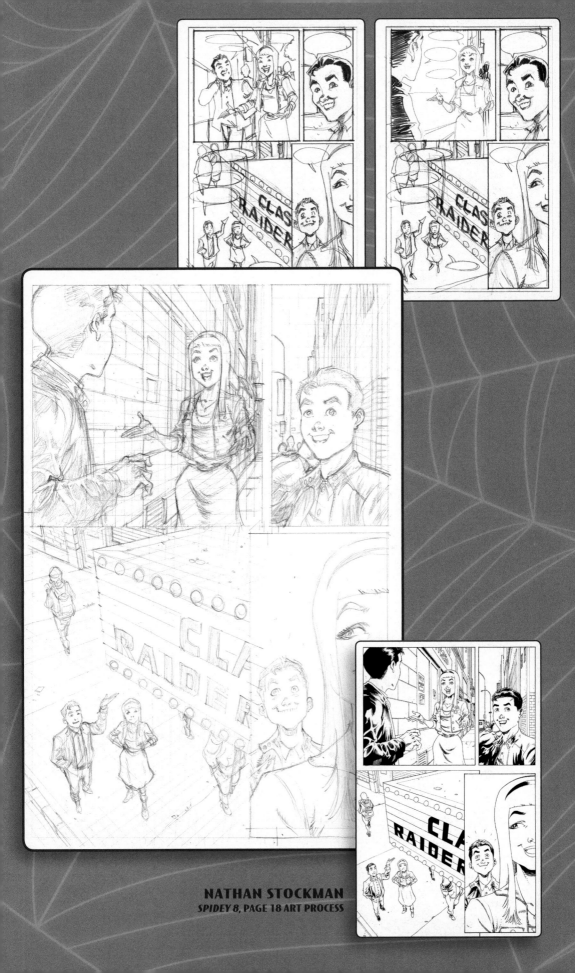

NATHAN STOCKMAN
SPIDEY 8, PAGE 18 ART PROCESS

NATHAN STOCKMAN
SPIDEY 8, PAGE 19 ART PROCESS

NATHAN STOCKMAN
SPIDEY 11, PAGE 2 ART PROCESS

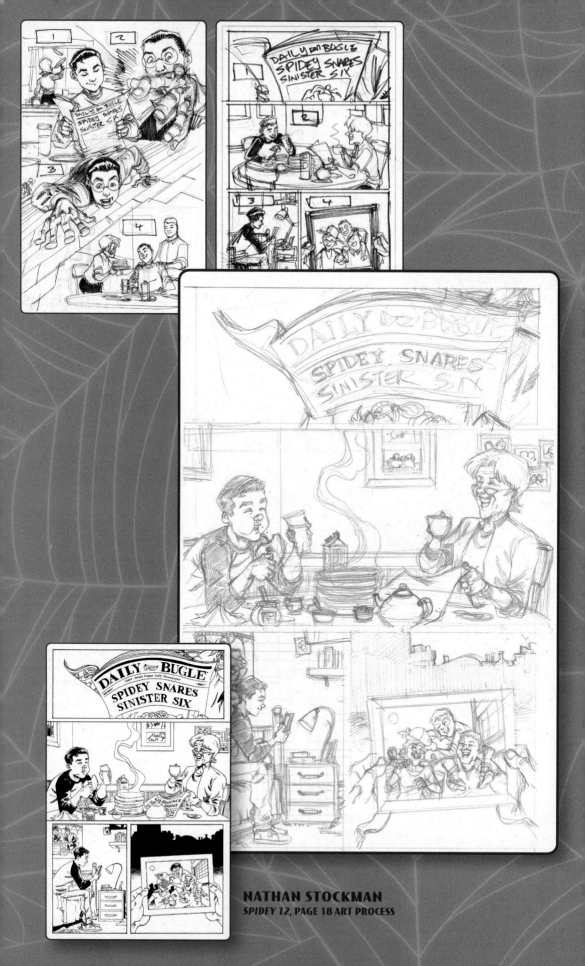

NATHAN STOCKMAN
SPIDEY 12, PAGE 18 ART PROCESS